The

Desert Fathers

VINTAGE SPIRITUAL CLASSICS

General Editors
John F. Thornton
Susan B. Varenne

ALSO AVAILABLE

The Imitation of Christ
The Little Flowers of St. Francis of Assisi
The Rule of St. Benedict

The
Desert Fathers

TRANSLATIONS

FROM THE LATIN WITH

AN INTRODUCTION BY

Helen Waddell

VINTAGE SPIRITUAL CLASSICS

VINTAGE BOOKS
A DIVISION OF RANDOM HOUSE, INC.
NEW YORK

A VINTAGE SPIRITUAL CLASSICS ORIGINAL, MAY 1998
FIRST EDITION

Library of Congress Cataloging-in-Publication Data
Vitae patrum. English.
The desert fathers : translations from the Latin / with an
introduction by Helen Waddell ; with a new introduction
by M. Basil Pennington.
p. cm. — (Vintage spiritual classics)
Originally published: London : Constable, 1936.
Includes bibliographical references.
ISBN 0-375-70019-6
1. Christian biography—Egypt. 2. Desert Fathers. 3. Christian saints—
Egypt. 4. Spiritual life—Christianity. I. Waddell, Helen, 1889–1965.
II. Title. III. Series.
BR1705.A2V525 1998
270.1—dc21 97-46372
CIP

www.randomhouse.com

Book design by Fritz Metsch

Printed in the United States of America
10 9 8 7 6 5 4 3 2 1

CONTENTS

CONTENTS

ABOUT THE
VINTAGE SPIRITUAL CLASSICS

by John F. Thornton and Susan B. Varenne, *General Editors*

A turn or shift of sorts is becoming evident in the reflections of men and women today on their life experiences. Not quite as adamantly secular and, perhaps, a little less insistent on material satisfactions, the reading public has recently developed a certain attraction to testimonies that human life is leavened by a Presence that blesses and sanctifies. Recovery, whether from addictions or personal traumas, illness, or even painful misalignments in human affairs, is evolving from the standard therapeutic goal of enhanced self-esteem. Many now seek a deeper healing that embraces the whole person, including the soul. Contemporary books provide accounts of the invisible assistance of angels. The laying on of hands in prayer has made an appearance at the hospital bedside. Guides for the spiritually perplexed have risen to the top of best-seller lists. The darkest shadows of skepticism and unbelief, which have eclipsed the presence of the Divine in our rational age, are beginning to lighten and part.

If the power and presence of God are real and effective, what do they mean for human experience? What does He offer to men and women, and what does He ask in return? How do we recognize Him? Know Him? Respond to Him? God has a reputation for being both benevolent and wrathful. Which will He be for me and when? Can these aspects of the Divine somehow be reconciled? Where is God when I suffer? Can I lose Him? Is God truthful, and are His promises to be trusted?

Are we really as precious to God as we are to ourselves and our loved ones? Do His providence and amazing grace guide our faltering steps toward Him, even in spite of ourselves? Will God abandon us if the sin is serious enough, or if we have episodes of resistance and forgetfulness? These are fundamental questions any person might address to God during a lifetime. They are pressing and difficult, often becoming wounds in the soul of the person who yearns for the power and courage of hope, especially in stressful times.

The Vintage Spiritual Classics present the testimony of writers across the centuries who have considered all these difficulties and who have pondered the mysterious ways, unfathomable mercies, and deep consolations afforded by God to those who call upon Him from out of the depths of their lives. These writers, then, are our companions, even our champions, in a common effort to discern the meaning of God in personal experience. For God is personal to us. To whom does He speak if not to us, provided we have the desire to hear Him deep within our hearts?

Each volume opens with a specially commissioned essay by a well-known contemporary writer that offers the reader an appreciation of its intrinsic value. A chronology of the general historical context of each work is provided, as are suggestions for further reading.

We offer a final word about the act of reading these spiritual classics. From the very earliest accounts of monastic practice—dating back to the fourth century—it is evident that a form of reading called *lectio divina* ("divine" or "spiritual reading") was essential to any deliberate spiritual life. This kind of reading is quite different from that of scanning a text for useful facts and bits of information, or advancing along an exciting plot line to a climax in the action. It is, rather, a meditative approach, by which the reader seeks to taste and savor the beauty and truth of every phrase and passage. This process of contemplative reading has the effect of enkindling in the reader compunction for past behavior that has been less than beautiful and true. At the same time, it increases the desire to seek a realm where all that is lovely and unspoiled may be found. There are four steps in *lectio divina*: first to read, next to meditate, then to rest in the sense of God's nearness, and, ultimately, to resolve to govern one's actions in the light of new understanding. This kind of reading is itself an act of prayer. And, indeed, it is in prayer that God manifests His Presence to us.

PREFACE TO THE
VINTAGE SPIRITUAL CLASSICS
EDITION

by M. Basil Pennington, O.C.S.O.

It is indeed an honor to be asked to add a new introduction to a book already blessed with the eloquent and erudite introduction of Helen Waddell, so rich in literary associations. At the same time it is quite humbling. But perhaps a simple, more pragmatic word might be useful to the average reader to make this rich contribution from our living Christian tradition more immediately relevant to his or her own journey in the realm of the Spirit. The value of this literature is not to know it or to know about it but to know that it was *lived* and to incorporate its values into our own lives.

As the fourth century unfolded, it seemed like Christianity was finally gaining some respectability. Yet in this same fourth century, to many in the Mediterranean area it seemed like the whole fabric of society was coming apart. The Roman Empire was splitting in two as barbarian hordes threatened it on every side, though which threatened Christian life more—the new respectability or the barbarian—it would be hard to say. The Founder's dictum "Render unto Caesar the things that are Caesar's and unto God the things that are God's" was more and more difficult to follow as taxes soared, ever-increasing military service was demanded, and a worldly Christianity began to flourish at the court and elsewhere in the Empire.

It is not surprising, then, that the desert began to receive devout Christians, inspired by the example of John the Baptizer—of whom "there was none greater born of woman"—and of the Master himself, who spent forty days in the desert before he began his public ministry.

When the young Alexandrine Anthony heard afresh the words "Go, sell what you have and follow me," he did just that. At first he disposed of the greater part of his wealth, saving only a portion to ensure care for his sister, and withdrew to the outer edges of the city. But again the evangelical word resounded in his soul, and he sold all he had, placed his sister in competent hands, and went forth into the desert. He was not the first there; he encountered the ancient Paul, but Patriarch Athanasius's *Life of Anthony* led to his being the most influential example.

As the fourth century progressed, the desert became increasingly peopled, first by hermits, who often grouped themselves in loosely connected associations, and then by cenobites, that is, monks who lived in organized communities, often guided by the rules developed by the saintly Pachomius. Besides the many who went to the desert to settle, the latter part of the century began to see a steady flow of pilgrims, seeking to be edified by immediate contact with these already fabled saints and to partake of their wisdom. Not only did these pilgrims write accounts of their journeys, giving us many colorful details from the lives of the fathers and mothers of the desert, but men like John Cassian sought to retain their wisdom in collections of conferences and sayings.

The wisdom of the desert enshrined in these varied writings continued to flow through Western Christian life even during what has been called the Dark Ages, and it shed a strong light on the renaissance the Church experienced as it moved into the glorious twelfth century. But with the last of the Fathers, Bernard of Clairvaux and his contemporaries, the patristic age came to a final close. Then the era of medieval scholasticism, perhaps drier than the deserts of the Fathers, began to hold sway. There were moments when the desert fathers were heard again, as with de Rancé in the seventeenth century, but for the most part this wisdom lay dormant during the whole of the scholastic parenthesis.

With the inspired renewal of our century, welcoming again the full humanism of the patristic age, there was a new hearing for the wisdom of the desert. In this, as in so much else, Helen Waddell was in the forefront, decades before such a call came from the Church-shaking Second Vatican Council. A Spirit-filled woman, she recognized how much of the wisdom of the Spirit is incarnated in the sayings and lives of the fathers and mothers of the desert. Powerfully, effectively, and practically, she has made it available to us.

At first one might feel the heroic way of these desert giants is too far removed from the quest of the everyday seeker living in this world's society. However, the fathers and mothers themselves, along with their early historians, sought to make it clear to us that this is not the case. Noteworthy in this regard is the rather lengthy account in the chapter entitled "History of the Monks of Egypt" of the last days of the fabled desert hermit Abba Paphnutius. We are told that as his end approached he "entreated the Lord that He would show him his like upon earth." And whom did the Lord show the saintly father? A street musician who had been a thief, the very busy headman of a local village, and a wealthy Alexandrine merchant. The historian goes on to tell us that, as the priests gathered around the dying saint, he told them:

All that the Lord had revealed to him, saying to them that no one in this world ought to be despised, let him be a thief, or an actor on the stage, or one that tilled the ground, and was bound to a wife, or was a merchant and served a trade: for in every condition of human life there are souls that please God and have their hidden deeds wherein He takes delight: whence is it plain that it is not so much profession or habit that is pleasing to God as the sincerity and affection of the soul and honesty of deed. And when he had spoken thus about each in turn, he gave up his spirit.

The final word of a great and saintly father—a teaching could not be given greater emphasis.

Everyone baptized into Christ, every true seeker, is called to the freedom of the children of God. This was essentially the quest of the desert: freedom—to be free to be oneself, to be who we truly are, to celebrate our oneness in our common humanity and in our call to share in the bliss of the divinity.

What is most evident and distinctive about these fathers and mothers is that they went apart, that they shunned a society that placed its values in the goods of this world and in prestige in their transient society. Most of us cannot go apart so radically, but we do need to separate ourselves from enslavement to this world's values. We may have to be in the world, but we cannot be of the world. Yes, render unto Caesar the things that are Caesar's, but render unto God, as fully and completely as we can, the things that are God's. This is the clearest witness of the men and women who fled from an increasingly worldly Church to the freedom of the desert.

This is no easy journey. Even if we were to spend as much time at the Lord's feet reading the Scriptures as we do watching the TV enthroned in our home, it would still be a losing battle.

For the TV is armed by the masters of the art of persuasion and all the sophistication of the ever-more modern media, and it calls forth as its ally the incalculable pressure of our peers to win us over to its hierarchy of values. It is only by the powerful grace of the Spirit that the Word of God, a double-edged sword, can pierce through and separate our spirit from the clutches of the worldly spirit. And that Holy Spirit will operate within as a liberating force only if we seek and welcome it. As a desert father of this century, Thomas Merton, put it: "Today, more than ever, we need to recognize that the gift of solitude is not ordered to the acquisition of strange, contemplative powers, but, first of all, to the recovery of one's deep self, and to the renewal of an authenticity which is presently twisted out of shape by the pretentious routines of a disordered togetherness."

Each of us needs to carve out some time apart to escape from the bombardment of the world and come to our true self. Our place apart can be a corner of our room where Bible or icon proclaim a Presence. Our going apart could mean just turning our chair away from our desk with all its affairs, leaving the world behind for a few minutes while we rest in the Presence and know ourselves to be held in a great and tender love. Or we may find our going apart in a short walk to a church, a library, or a park—some spot where we can sit for a bit in the quietness and know something of the *quies* of the desert.

The men and women of the desert wanted the liberating force of the Spirit to have the greatest possible freedom to work in their lives. So they went apart, separating themselves from the society of this world. Most of the fathers and mothers we hear of in these pages went so far as to shun even the society of fellow monks or nuns in the monastic communities that were coming into being in this period. They went apart to their solitary cells. But they were not haters of their fellow humans. It is

noteworthy that in her magnificent introduction the first stories
Helen Waddell recalls are of compassion, care, and mercy. As
examples of these traits, the men and women of the desert were
absolutely outstanding. Story after story, saying after saying, be-
speaks these fundamental virtues, this expression of a Christlike
love. The fathers and mothers showed an immensely loving and
truly touching care not only for the newcomers who came into
their midst and for the venerable ancients among them but for
any troubled one. Edifying, to say the least, was their response to
visitors, whether they were humble seekers, true pilgrims, or
just the curious and those who wanted to go home and tell their
story. One cannot help but be touched by the ready way in
which these desert dwellers set aside their own much-loved
practices and their precious solitude to welcome these visitors
and make them as comfortable as their limited means and in-
hospitable setting allowed. I think if I had to fasten on one single virtue to ascribe preeminently to these women and men, it
would be the virtue of compassion. The author of the "History
of the Monks of Egypt" expresses this beautifully:

> But of their humanity, their courtesy, their loving-kindness,
> what am I to say, when each man of them would have brought us
> into his own cell, not only to fulfil the due of hospitality, but still
> more out of humbleness, wherein they are indeed masters, and
> from gentleness and its kindred qualities which are learned
> among them with diverse grace but one and the same doctrine,
> as if they had come apart from the world for this same end.
> Nowhere have I seen love so in flower, nowhere so quick com-
> passion, or hospitality so eager.

I think another surprising element in the lives of these solitaries is their very real and practical concern for the poor. They

took to heart the Lord's description of the judgment in Matthew 25 and sought to feed the hungry Christ and clothe him and even leave their solitude to go into the city to visit him in prison. In their solitary cells monks would weave extra baskets or mats to be sold for the benefit of the poor. During the harvest season some of them would even hire themselves out to farmers along the Nile in order to earn money for the poor. And from their own harvest they sent a good bit of produce to the poor in the cities while contenting themselves with very little. Certainly they challenge us all to consider what indeed we are doing to feed, to clothe, to comfort, and to care.

The fathers and mothers of the desert exemplify for us in so many, many ways a true hierarchy of values and balance in their practice of the virtuous life. If there are reports of exaggerations and distortions—and some writers have always been prone to make these the substance of their reports—these tales join the edifying accounts in teaching through their contrast and through their evidence of the rejection of such activity by all the holier and wiser of the fathers and mothers.

The "Sayings of the Fathers," those rough-hewn words of life or words of salvation that cut so ruthlessly through all our pretenses, make up the bulk of this volume. And that is well. They are far more precious than the sometimes starry-eyed, always colored accounts of the pilgrims and storytellers. These sayings are very nearly if not actually the words that passed through the desert wastes from the lips of one disciple to another, once they fell from the lips of some revered father or mother. Their jagged angularity has its audacious way of intruding with a cutting edge into some of our most sacred preserves. As the great Barsanufius wrote to Archimandrite Dorotheos: "For those capable of understanding these words and keeping them, there is joy and great profit."

An eagerness for a "word of life" should mark every Christian. We can with great profit turn to the sayings gathered here and in other collections mentioned in "Suggestions for Further Reading." Or like the fathers and mothers themselves, we can turn to that ever-fruitful source, the Holy Scriptures. The author of the "History of the Monks in Egypt," with perhaps a bit of enthusiastic exaggeration, tells of the monks' and nuns' eagerness in this regard: "And nowhere have I seen such meditation upon Holy Writ or understanding of it, or such discipline of sacred learning: wellnigh might you judge each one of them a doctor in the wisdom of God." A daily meeting with the Lord in the Gospels, as a true disciple seeking a word of life from the Master, is perhaps the surest way for each one of us to grow into the mind of Christ.

If we wanted a listing of the virtues we need to pursue in order to develop a full Christlike freedom, they come forth like a litany in the chapter headings of Pelagius and John's translation of the Greek collection: "Of Quiet . . . Of Compunction . . . Of Self-Restraint . . . Not to Be a Show-off . . . Not to Judge . . . Of Discretion . . . Of Sobriety . . . To Pray Without Ceasing . . . Hospitality and Mercy with Cheerfulness [how wonderful is that addition: "with Cheerfulness"!] . . . Of Obedience . . . Of Humility . . . Of Patience . . . Of Love . . . Of Contemplation." And for the practice of each, the sayings offer us some wise and challenging counsel.

The list begins and ends with the same goal: quiet or contemplation. The desert folk preferred the former word, so much less pretentious. And we might well be more comfortable with it, given all the baggage that has gathered around that term "contemplation." *Quies,* quiet—that wonderful freedom to be able to rest quietly in the Lord, knowing that in him we have all. No longer tugged this way and that by our passions, emotions, uncontrolled desires—this is what was behind all the austerity of the desert, what motivated it and encouraged the monks and nuns to persevere in it. They longed for the freedom to do what they really wanted to do, be who they wanted to be, without having constantly to struggle against thoughts—which for them included also all fantasies and feelings—that sought to master them and rule them.

We cannot hope to free ourselves from the false self that the values of this world encourage us to create, to escape the self-alienation that marks our lives from the womb and is constantly fostered by a worldly society, if we do not at times and even regularly seek periods of quietness. This is the goal of all authentic meditation practices and especially of the centering prayer that comes to us from this desert tradition—the quietness that enables us to be Christ to the Father in Holy Spirit.

But anyone who has practiced meditation knows that the asceticism of the practice requires us not only to give time to meditation but during the actual time of meditation to be faithful in setting aside thoughts, feelings, emotions, desires, all the expressions of the self. Herein is the true purpose of ascetic practice: to free ourselves from the imperious domination of our own thoughts, passions, and desires, to free the spirit for the things of the Spirit.

It is paradoxical, isn't it, that what seem to be life-denying practices actually open the space for new life. The men and women of the desert, who all but died to life in this world, found the way, already here and now, to enter into some participation in eternal life with its joy beyond earthly joy. These holy ones were largely skilled in hiding the more sublime workings of God within them, but between the lines and in their candid instruction to beloved disciples we catch glimmers of the fullness of life that they experienced. They certainly give witness to the reality of a life beyond this life—a richer, happier life. They tell us, more by the way they lived than by their wonderful words, that this life is to be lived more for that life than for this.

I think among all the stories found in this volume the one that has touched me most is the story of Nonnus and Pelagia. The revered bishop Nonnus was sitting in the porch of the cathedral of Antioch imparting words of life to the bishops assembled there. As he concluded his remarks, the beautiful Pelagia, the leading actress of the city, rode by, surrounded by her retinue, her body most beautifully adorned, "bare of head and shoulder and limb." The other bishops groaned with disdain and turned away. But the blessed Nonnus "did long and most intently regard her: and after she had passed by still he gazed and still his eyes went after her." He then questioned his fellow bishops: "Did not the sight of her great beauty delight you?" Not one answered a word. He went on to say, "Verily, it greatly delighted me, and well pleased was I with her beauty." The wonderful ability to see, enjoy, and praise the beauty of God's creation wherever it is to be found, this too was a mark of the holiest and wisest of the fathers and mothers. The saintly bishop even added, "whom God shall set in presence of His high and terrible seat, in judgment of ourselves and our episcopate."

After saying this the bishop went on to draw what for me was a powerful lesson:

What think you, beloved? How many hours hath this woman spent in her chamber, bathing and adorning herself with all solicitude and all her mind on the stage, that there may be no stain or flaw in all that body's beauty and its wearing, that she may be a joy to all men's eyes, nor disappoint those paltry lovers of hers who are but for a day and tomorrow are not? And we who have in heaven a Father Almighty, an immortal Lover, with the promise of riches eternal and rewards beyond all reckoning, since eye hath not seen nor ear hath heard nor hath it ascended into the heart of man to conceive the things that God hath prepared for them that love Him—but what need is there of further speech? With such a promise, the vision of the Bridegroom, that great and splendid and ineffable face, whereon the Cherubim dare not look, we adorn not, we care not so much as to wash the filth from our miserable souls, but leave them lying in their squalor.

The saintly bishop does indeed challenge us!

For the rest of the story of the bishop and the harlot, turn back to Helen Waddell's beautiful translation of "The Life of St. Pelagia the Harlot."

And if, after you have been nourished by the choice and tasty selections found in this slender volume, you would like some more of this hearty food, a few suggestions may be found at the end of the book.

CHRONOLOGY OF
THE DESERT FATHERS
150 B.C.–400 A.D.

Pre-Christian Monasticism

150 B.C.–68 A.D. The Essenes/Qumranites were a pre-Christian religious sect of Jewish Palestinians who lived ascetic lives in small communities on the west shore of the Dead Sea. They practiced fervent, rigorous observance of the Torah in expectation of a Davidic/Aaronic Messiah. The Dead Sea Scrolls, first discovered in the caves near Qumran in 1947, detail the rules of the community life of the Essenes. It is possible that John the Baptist, son of Zechariah and Elizabeth and cousin to Jesus, was influenced by the desert asceticism of the Essenes, who lived very near the Jordan, where he administered his baptism of repentance.

Life of Jesus: Desert Sojourn

ca. 27 A.D. At the beginning of Jesus' public life, after his baptism in the river Jordan by John, he went into the desert alone to pray. Accounts are given in the gospels of Matthew (4:1–11), Mark (1:12–13), and Luke (4:1–13) of Jesus' solitary forty-day retreat. During this time he fasted, prayed, and endured temptations by Satan, who tried to seduce him with promises of material power and prosperity if he would disobey God and worship

Satan instead. Jesus refused Satan and affirmed his obedience to the will of his Father.

Jesus was tested in ways analogous to the tribe of Israel during its years of wandering in the desert after the escape from slavery in Egypt. Moses had spent forty days on Mount Sinai in prayer, after which he received the revelation of the Ten Commandments from God. In the desert Israel was asked to affirm its obedience in faith to Yahweh, who manifested Himself to them as the one, true God, and who gave His law as a guide. The Israelites were repeatedly tempted to abandon Yahweh for pagan idol worship before they finally arrived in the Promised Land, a paradigm of heaven.

Primitive Christian Spirituality and Asceticism

100–400 A.D. Early Christian, premonastic spirituality included fasting, voluntary celibacy, community prayer, and simple living. Wealth and security in this life were eschewed by ardent followers as a way of identifying with the sufferings of the poor Christ. Renunciation of the things of this world allowed devout Christians to focus their hearts and minds on the Kingdom of God and the Second Coming of Christ. The origins of Christian monasticism are in the Gospels. From the earliest days of Christianity, some men and some women have wanted to lead lives entirely consecrated to God by following the example and teachings of Christ.

Members of the primitive Church gathered together for the eucharistic supper, which included homilies on Scripture readings and prayers. These early years of the Church were marked by persecution. To accept baptism was to incur the risk of martyrdom. To die in the name of Christ and for His sake was to imitate Him with the totality of one's being.

285–337 A.D. Persecution ceased under Constantine the Great, the Roman emperor who was converted to Christianity through the influence of his mother, St. Helena. By the fourth century, peace and security allowed a certain political and material worldliness to influence Christian life. This in turn gave rise to the impetus for some to flee society for the desert in search of a more pure and intense life of prayer and asceticism.

Egyptian Desert Monasticism—The Desert Fathers

ca. 250–400 A.D. The first solitary hermits, later to be known as the Desert Fathers, left the material comforts, worldly politics, and secular social distractions of urban Egyptian life for the forbidding solitude of the Nile desert region. There they led lives of uninterrupted prayer and great physical mortification. Some women also withdrew from the world, and they too lived as anchorites. Now that the Church and the State were at peace, the ideal of martyrdom, or dedication unto death for the faith, gave way to an ideal of asceticism as a substitute for the shedding of one's blood.

ca. 227–340 St. Paul of Thebes is commonly called the first Christian hermit. For ninety years Paul lived in a cave, dedicating himself to prayer and mortification in quest of purity of heart. His life was an expression of longing for the innocence of Paradise before the sin of Adam.

ca. 251–356 St. Anthony of Egypt heard the Gospel call to give all his possessions to the poor and so disposed of his wealth and retired to the desert in 285, determined not to let the desire for possessions rule his life. He became known as the "father of all monks" when St. Athanasius, who was bishop of Alexandria in

Egypt, wrote his biography. This document of primitive monastic life details the asceticism of evangelical perfection: withdrawal from the world, renunciation, solitude, work, and prayer, which are the foundation of the monk's life even today. This description of anchoritic monastic life was translated into Latin (*Vita Antonii*) and became well-known and influential in the West.

ca. 290–346 St. Pachomius was born of pagan parents and received baptism when he was serving as a soldier. After his conversion he left the army and gave himself over to a life of desert asceticism. He soon proposed that the monks living as hermits come together to eat and to share the fruits of their labors. Eventually these monks adopted similar dress, which included a tunic of linen, a cloak of goat skin, and a hood to cover the head. Their common life evolved into a walled enclosure, which included a church, refectory, dormitory, garden, and a separate lodging for visitors. In 404 A.D., St. Jerome translated the *Rule of Pachomius* into Latin. This rule contains directives for living a monastic common life based on fellowship in the Eucharist such as was found in the very early Christian communities. The *Rule* had a profound influence on succeeding forms of Western monasticism.

ca. 329–379 St. Basil the Great founded monastic communities in Cappadocia, eastern Asia Minor, which he oriented to a life in common. His *Rule,* influenced by that of St. Pachomius, incorporated the asceticism of consecrated virginity and poverty. St. Basil also insisted on liturgical prayer, confession of sins, frequent reception of the Eucharist, reading of the Bible, manual labor, and good works such as hospitality, care of the sick, and teaching, all of which were governed by obedience to the authority of the abbot. St. Benedict of Nursia, who wrote his own famous rule around 530 A.D., was known to send his more experienced monks back to the *Rule of St. Basil.*

It is through the linkage of such influences that the impulse to monastic living—a life in common of prayer, celibacy, obedience, and good works—can be traced to its very wellspring: the life of Jesus Himself as recounted in the Gospels of the New Testament.

The

Desert Fathers

INTRODUCTION

by Helen Waddell

I

Sometime toward the end of the year, for the closing of the seas was near at hand, and sometime in the last decades of his own life, Athanasius, Archbishop of Alexandria, wrote the preface to the life of his friend Antony, the first of the Fathers of the Desert. It was intended for the *fratres pergrinos,* the brethren from overseas, the instancy of whose letters had brought Athanasius to set down what he knew. He had meant, he says, to ask some of the monks who knew Antony best to visit him, so that he could have written from fuller knowledge and made a better book of it: but the *tempora navigationis,* the sailing season, was slipping past, and the bearer of the letters was in a violent hurry, so that he has had to make shift with his own memories ("for I visited him often"). Antony had indeed remembered him on his deathbed. He had begged his two disciples to save his body from a thing most abhorrent to him, the Egyptian rites of the dead. "Shelter in the ground, hide in the earth the body of your father: and let you do your old man's bidding [*vestri seni*] in this also, that none but your love only shall know the place of my grave." He had turned then to the disposition of the other worn-out garments of his spirit. "The sheepskin and the old cloak I am lying on give to Athanasius the bishop; he brought it to me new. Let Serapion the bishop have the other sheepskin: do you take my haircloth, and farewell, ye that are my heartstrings, for Antony is going, and will not be with you in this world any more." They kissed him, and he, "stretching out his feet a little, looked joyously on death."[1]

Some years later, Evagrius of Antioch, to whom even St. Jerome admitted a keen intelligence,[2] translated the Life into Latin for the benefit of those who had no Greek, deploring as he did so the enfeebling (*infirmitatem*) that the energy of the Greek tongue suffers in entering the Latin. It was a free translation, and in his brief preface to his friend Innocent he wrote the charter of liberties for his successors. "Direct word for word translation from one language into another darkens the sense and strangles it, even as spreading couchgrass a field of corn. . . . For my part, to avoid this, I have so transposed this life of the Blessed Antony which you desired that whatever lack may be in the words, there is none in the meaning. Let the rest go bat-fowling for letters and syllables: do you seek for the sense."[3]

It was through this translation that Antony of Egypt was given the freedom of Latin Europe, and fifteen centuries later was to find Flaubert and Anatole France among his disciples, latecomers, but not the least in affection; France indeed observing his every gesture with the attentive and innocent eye of a robin. But within thirty years of his death (for Augustine was told the story in 386) a manuscript of the *Vitæ* had made its way to a small house outside the walls of Trèves, where a few poor brothers lived the common life. The Emperor was in residence, but on this afternoon had gone to the races, and four of his staff had taken advantage of it to set out on a country walk. They fell as they walked into pairs, as four men will, and two of them, sauntering through the gardens outside the city walls, came on the little house and without ceremony went in. One of them picked up the book and began to read. "Let no one who hath renounced the world think that he hath given up some great thing . . . the whole earth set over against heaven's infinite is scant and poor. . . ."[4] As he read, ambition fell from him: about him was the

> "twilight air
> That has made anchorites of kings."

He spoke with his friend, no less shaken than he: and now the other two came up with talk of going home: they had been everywhere through the orchards looking for them, and it was near sunset. They were told the story, but good devout men as they were, their hearts dragged to earth, and they went back to the Palace. But the young men stayed in that poor house, and in a little while the sweethearts that they had, when they too heard the story, took the same vow.

Some time after, in the late summer of 386, Pontician, still a distinguished civil servant, came to visit his friends Augustine and Alypius in Milan. He was, like them, from North Africa, and the three sat down to talk. A book lay beside him on a *mensam lusoriam* (as it might be a card-table), and he picked it up, thinking it one of the textbooks that Augustine was using in his lectures on rhetoric: it was near the end of term, within three weeks of the holidays for the vintage. The book was the Epistles of St. Paul, and the courtly eyebrows lifted, for whatever his personal devotion, he had not associated his friend Augustine with that kind of reading. Augustine protested that he had been spending a good deal of time upon it: and from that Pontician fell to talk of Antony, of whom neither of his friends had ever heard, and from Antony, of that rich solitude of the Desert, to which so many men were now being drawn. He told the story of the codex in the little house outside Trèves, and how sorrowfully he himself had turned his back on it and come away. Augustine sat, knowing that the thing to which he listened was that which he had sought and fled from for twelve years, "that whereof not the finding but the sole seeking is beyond the treasuries of kings and all this ambient bodily delight." He sat in silence, and his soul quailed away from it as from death.

Pontician took his leave, and Augustine, starting up with a cry, went from the house out into the garden, to the ultimate agony of the will. They came about him, plucking at him, the trifling, heedless pleasures of his daily use, the dear indulgence of the unthinking flesh: *"And dost thou send us away?"* and *"From this moment we shall never be with thee, to all eternity, any more."* There came to him the memory of how a single sentence heard one day had sent Antony into poverty and solitude: for he had great possessions. "Go and sell all that thou hast and give to the poor, and thou shalt have treasure in heaven: and come and follow me." He came back to the seat in the garden where he had thrown down his St. Paul, and opened it at random. "'Not in rioting and drunkenness, not in chambering and wantonness, not in strife and envying: but put ye on the Lord Jesus Christ and make no provision for the flesh to fulfil the lusts thereof.' I had no mind to read further; nor was there need."[5]

Antony had gone to the desert: but there Augustine did not follow him. It was not the inhuman austerities, the demon-haunted vigils, impressive as they were to the grosser imagination of his age, that moved him: it was the secret renunciation, the doctrine of the power of the will. "Fear not," Antony had said, "this goodness as a thing impossible, nor the pursuit of it as something alien, set a great way off: it hangeth on our own arbitrament. For the sake of the Greek learning men go overseas . . . but the city of God hath its foundations in every seat of human habitation . . . the Kingdom of God is within. . . . The goodness that is in us doth ask but the human mind."[6] It asked and found in Augustine the richest mind in Christendom.

II

"If I may be permitted to use strong language," wrote Harnack, "I should not hesitate to say that no book has had a more stultifying (*verdummender*) effect on Egypt, Western Asia, and Europe than the *Vita S. Antonii*." Antony was buried in 356: in his own lifetime and for more than a hundred years after his death men were flocking for religion to the desert, as eight hundred years later they flocked for philosophy to Paris, and to Bologna for law. Pachomius, from his monastery of Tabenna in the Nile, had seven thousand men and women living in various congregations under his rule: there were five thousand monks on Mount Nitria: Serapion at Arsinoë ruled over ten thousand: and a traveller through Egypt and Palestine about 394 reports the dwellers in the desert as all but equal to the population of the towns.[7] Enthusiasm has an indifferent head for figures: but with every qualification the movement was formidable enough in its incidence on civilisation to excite the slow-dropping malice of Gibbon, and the more human distress of Lecky. "There is perhaps no phase in the moral history of mankind of a deeper or more painful interest than this ascetic epidemic. A hideous, distorted and emaciated maniac, without knowledge, without patriotism, without natural affection, spending his life in a long routine of useless and atrocious self-torture, and quailing before the ghastly phantoms of his delirious brain, had become the ideal of the nations which had known the writings of Plato and Cicero and the lives of Socrates and Cato." It is superb invective, with that note, not of the sunken church bell, but of the sunken pulpit, that no nineteenth-century prose, however rationalist, can drown. And it is with this comminatory surge in his ears that the average reader opens the *Vitae Patrum,* the massive seventeenth-century folio in which Rosweyde collected the scattered fragments of the lives and sayings of the Desert Fathers.

"The place called Scete is set in a vast desert, a day and a night from the monasteries on Nitria; and it is reached by no path, nor is the track shown by any landmarks of earth, but one journeys by the signs and courses of the stars. Water is hard to find. . . . Here abide men perfect in holiness (for so terrible a place can be endured by none save those of absolute resolve and supreme constancy); yet is their chief concern the loving kindness which they show to one another and towards such as by chance may reach that spot. . . ."

"At one time the Abbot John was climbing up from Scete with other brethren: and he who was by way of guiding them mistook the way, for it was night. And the brethren said to the Abbot John, 'What shall we do, Father, for the brother has missed the way and we may lose ourselves and die?' And the old man said, 'If we say aught to him, he will be cast down. But I shall make a show of being worn out, and say that I cannot walk, but must lie here till morning.' And he did so. And the others said, 'Neither shall we go on: but shall sit down beside thee.' And they sat down until morning, so as not to discountenance their brother. . . ."

"A certain brother had sinned and the priest commanded him to go out from the church. But Bessarion rose up and went out with him, saying, 'I too am a sinful man.' . . ."

"There is another place in the inner desert . . . called Cellia. To this spot those who have had their first initiation and who desire to live a remoter life, stripped of all its trappings, withdraw themselves: for the desert is vast, and the cells are sundered from one another by so wide a space that none is in sight of his neighbour, nor can any voice be heard. One by one they abide in their cells, a mighty silence and a great quiet among them: only on the Saturday and on the Sunday do they come together to church, and there they see each other face to face as folk restored in heaven. If by chance any one is missing in that gathering, straightway they understand that he has been detained by some unevenness of his body, and they all go to visit him, not indeed all of them together but at different times and each carrying with him whatever he may have by him at home that might seem grateful to the sick. But for no other cause dare any disturb the silence of his neighbour. . . ."

"The abbot Marcus said to the abbot Arsenius, 'Wherefore dost thou flee from us?' And the old man said, 'God knows that I love you: but I cannot be with God and with men. A thousand and a thousand thousand of the angelic powers have one will: and men have many. Wherefore I cannot send God from me and come and be with men.'"[8]

> "Look up a-height: the shrill-gorged lark so far
> Cannot be heard."

It is the plainness of the fourth century, over against the civility of the eighteenth, the humanism of the nineteenth, the common sense of the twentieth: and it is dangerous.

> "Into my heart an air that kills
> From yon far country blows."

Yet there is another voice from that century, and it speaks a very different language. Rutilius Claudius Namatianus, son of a

curial house in Southern France, was one of the scanty fellowship who stood with Symmachus

—*O pereuntum*
assertor divum. . . .[9]

last protestants for the dying gods. But not even Symmachus
with his golden throat could bring back the Altar of Victory to
the Senate House: and with Theodosius in his grave, there was
no one to go out with the eagles. Symmachus was already dead
before Rome fell to the barbarians in 410: but his younger
henchman lived to see her sacked and still inviolate, and to write
her the last great invocation in Latin verse, as his galley, bound
for Marseilles, stood out to sea. Rather more than five centuries
later,

O Roma nobilis, orbis et domina—

"O Rome that noble art, and the world's lady . . .
Red with the ruby and rose of the martyrs,
White with the lilies and light of the virgins—"[10]

was chanted along the pilgrim roads: but in a metre that Rutilius would have found as abominable as the sentiments and character of the singers.

Meantime, "marching of the sea" had brought him past the
north-east coast of Corsica and the rocks of Capraja, an island
once inhabited by goats but sadly altered of late. For a monastery
now stood upon it, and at sight of it, "squalid with fugitives from
light," Rutilius roused to a scorning elegiac fury beside which
Gibbon's malice shows of a sudden spinsterish and thin.

"Make thyself wretched, lest thou mayst be wretched. . . .
O foolish frenzy of a perverse brain,
Trembling at ill, intolerant of good.
'Tis conscience turns them executioners,
Or dismal guts distended with black gall."[11]

Capraja sinks: but after an interval of fifty lines, Gorgona rises, a craggy islet where a sometime friend now lived an anchorite, and Rutilius' disgust quickens into a more generous anger for the waste of youth and hope. For he was a young man, *noster invenis,* this creature who now is undergoing living burial,

"Driven by the furies, out from men and lands,
A credulous exile skulking in the dark,
Thinking, poor fool, that Heaven feeds on filth,
Himself to himself more harsh than the outraged gods.
A worse creed this than ever Circe's poison,
Men's bodies then turned bestial, now their souls."[12]

Now, it is agreeable to reflect that this admirable invective owes its survival to its preservation in a single manuscript by the monks of Bobbio. The first edition appeared at Bologna in 1520: another, by Barth, in 1623, was enlivened by the editor's description of the author as one of the *canes rabiosi diaboli,* the devil's mad dogs. But it is for a poet to counter a poet: and an answer that would have turned away even Rutilius' wrath had been written twenty years before him by a man of the same tradition, like him of a great French house, an accomplished scholar, ex-senator, ex-consul, and finally parish priest of Nola: who even as Rutilius sailed for Marseilles was living in poverty after spending the last of a royal fortune in ransoming the prisoners taken in the sack of Rome.

"Not that they beggared be in mind, or brutes,
That they have chosen a dwelling-place afar
In lonely places: but their eyes are turned
To the high stars, the very deep of Truth.
Freedom they seek, and emptiness apart
From worthless hopes: din of the market place
And all the noisy crowding up of things,
And whatsoever wars on the Divine,
At Christ's command and for His love, they hate.
By faith and hope they follow after God,
And know their quest shall not be desperate,
If but the Present conquer not their souls
With hollow things: that which they see they spurn,
That they may come at what they do not see,
Their senses kindled like a torch that may
Blaze through the secrets of eternity.
The transient's open, everlastingness
Denied our sight: yet still by hope we follow
The vision that our eyes have seen, despising
The shows and forms of things, the loveliness
Soliciting for ill our mortal eyes.
The present's nothing: but eternity
Abides for those on whom all truth, all good,
Hath shone in one entire and perfect light."[13]

Yet Rutilius is not wholly answered: and there is solid foundation beneath Lecky's melancholy indictment. It is true that the
sensitive ear can catch in Rutilius' invective that high, shrill note
of righteous indignation which is the normal reaction of
mankind to a way of living—and indeed of writing—to which
it is not accustomed and which it does not understand: and that
Lecky is guilty for once of special pleading when he produced
his squalid maniac—presumably St. Simeon Stylites—as typical
of the discipline of the Desert. For that tormented and prepos-

terous figure belongs to the decadence. His more revolting practices, the very reading of which demands a strong and
insensitive stomach, are the most insane extravagances of
Eastern asceticism, and peculiar to no age and no creed. Inci-
dentally they made him extremely offensive to his more fastidi-
ous brethren. In his later life he had a fantastic success, and in
death a princely funeral: but thereafter his fame falls curiously
silent. He was never a household word in the Middle Ages, un-
like the kindly Antony, who in his progress down the centuries
acquired a pig (the legitimate property of his junior of Padua),
as Jerome his lion and donkey and Cardinal's hat. Not even a
lizard shared his pillar with St. Simeon: though a blinded
dragon is reported to have once visited its base and undergone
conversion.[14] His present reputation, vast as it is, dates largely
from the eighteenth century, and balances delicately on a paragraph of Gibbon's prose.

For the Desert, though it praised austerity, reckoned it
among the rudiments of holy living, and not as an end in itself:
asceticism had not travelled far from the *ascesis,* the training of
the athlete, and the Fathers themselves to their contemporary
biographers are the *athletae Dei,* the athletes of God. Human
passion, the passion of anger as well as of lust, entangled the life
of the spirit: therefore passion must be dug out by the roots.
"Our mind is hampered and called back from the contemplation of God, because we are led into captivity to the passions of
the flesh."[15] The actual words were spoken by the abbot
Theonas, but they echo sentence after sentence from Socrates in
the *Phaedo.* "Spirit must brand the flesh that it may live," said
George Meredith, who was no Puritan: and Dorotheus the The-
ban put it more bluntly fifteen hundred years earlier: "I kill my
body, for it kills me."[16] Moreover, the wisest of the Fathers dis-
countenanced publicity, dissembling both their moments of ec-

stasy and the meagreness of their fare.[17] The great Macarius, indeed, seems to have been moved for a while by the ill spirit of
competition. Did he hear that one Father ate only a pound of
bread, himself was content to nibble a handful of crusts: did another eat no cooked food for the forty days of Lent, raw herbs
became his diet for seven years. The fame of the high austerity
of Tabenna reached him in his fastness: he came fifteen days'
journey across the desert, disguised as a working man, inter-
viewed the abbot, the great and gentle Pachomius, and was admitted on probation with some ado, for he was an old man, said
the abbot, and not inured to abstinence like his own monks, who
had been trained to it, and would only end by going away with
a grievance and an ill word of the monastery. Lent was about to
begin: and having observed with an attentive eye the various activities of the brethren, how one brother chose to fast till vespers,
another for two days, another for five, how one stood up all
night and sat weaving his mats all day, Macarius proceeded to
combine these excellencies in one person. Providing himself
with plenty of palm-fibre steeped and ready for plaiting, he
stood himself in a corner for the forty days till Easter, neither
eating bread nor drinking water, nor kneeling nor lying, nor
sleeping nor speaking, but silently praying and efficiently plaiting, and, to avoid ostentation, eating a few raw cabbage leaves
on Sundays. The infuriated brethren came seething about their
abbot—it would seem that Pachomius had been disappointingly
unaware of the record performance being given in their
midst—demanding where he had found this creature without
human flesh who was bringing them all into contempt: either he
left, or they did, in one body, that same day. Pachomius heard
them out: he meditated, prayerfully, and the identity of his em-
barrassing visitor was suddenly revealed to him. He went to find
him, led him by the hand to his private oratory, and there kissed

him and greeted him by name, gently reproaching him for his efforts at disguise from one who had for many years desired to see him. "I give thee thanks that thou hast clouted the ears of these youngsters of mine [*quia colaphos nostris infantibus dedisti*], and put the conceit out of them. Now, therefore, return to the place from whence thou camest: we have all been sufficiently edified by thee: and pray for us."[18] Had I been in Macarius' shoes, said the abbé Brémond, I think I would have come out of that church less triumphant than I went in. The Desert was a school of high diplomacy as well as of devotion: and *Verba Seniorum* has something of the irony of the Gospels.

It is doubtful, however, if Palladius, who told that story, ever saw the point of it: for Palladius was a cheerful gossip, always ready to be impressed by the more obvious and picturesque activities of his elders, and in his first experience of the desert summed the popular view in one compendious phrase. He had gone from the kind nursery of Alexandria to learn continence under Dorotheus of Thebes for three years, but could not stay the course: the life of his master, he confessed, seemed to him "harsh, squalid, and exceeding dry."[19] Himself, in his own phrase, a bishop of pots and pans, quick to detect a wine that had gone sour and to drink a better,[20] he became a faithful Boswell to the more austere saints, and a wholehearted admirer of virtues not his own. But the more sensitive and intelligent observers, Cassian, the anonymous author of the *Historia Monachorum,* the compilers of the *Verba Seniorum,* were less moved by the *ascesis* and more by the harder virtues to which it led: magnanimity, humility, gentleness. The quintessence of the Desert is in the exquisite story, frugal as the light of its own dawn, of how Macarius, returning at daybreak with his bundle of palm-leaves, met the Evil One, and the Evil One feinted at him with his sickle, but could not reach him, and began to cry out on Macarius for the violence he did him. "Yet whatever thou dost, I do also, and more. Thou dost fast now and then, but by no food am I ever refreshed: thou dost often keep vigil, but no slumber ever falls upon me. In one thing only dost thou overmaster me." And when the saint asked what that might be, "In thy humility." And the saint fell on his knees—it may be to repel this last and subtlest temptation—and the devil vanished into the air.[21]

Yet the indictment of the life of the Desert is not to be dismissed for a single flaw in the evidence, a misdirection of the jury. The root of the quarrel between the humanists and the Desert is not the exact length to which the branding of the flesh may legitimately go. What ailed Rutilius and Gibbon and Lecky is the Roman civic conscience: and to the Roman civic conscience the exiles in the desert are deserters from a sinking ship, fugitives from a rotting civilisation, concerned only for their personal integrity. Augustine had the civic conscience: the sack of Rome sent him to his book of reconstruction, a city that had foundations, whose builder and maker is God, but a city that could be built on the rubble of the Empire, even as Blake would have built Jerusalem among the dark Satanic mills. "We are of God," the Desert seemed to say, "and the whole world lieth in wickedness." One of the oldest brief summaries of the Desert rule is the answer of an old man questioned as to what manner of man a monk should be: "So far as in me is, alone to the alone (*solus ad solum*).[22] "Except," said the abbot Allois, "a man shall say in his heart, I alone and God are in this world, he shall not find peace."[23]

Now this—profoundly true of the first encounter of the soul and God, though not of the ultimate adoration that burns up all knowledge of a man's self—is a kind of treason to the *civitas Dei*, nor does it represent the whole of the Desert teaching. "With our neighbour," said Antony, prince of solitaries, "is life and death."[24] But it has enough truth in it to shadow forth the supreme temptation for the saint, the artist, and the lover, the temptation of the narrow world that has room only for the saint and God, the artist and his subject, the lover and his beloved.

> "Who is so safe as we, where none can do
> Treason to us, except one of us two?"

Portus impassibilitatis, mansionem in terra quietorum praeparare,[25] the haven of invulnerable living, to build a house in the land of quiet men, phrases such as these do but make articulate the sighing of the prisoners of a clattering world, the last delusion of the human heart that solitude is peace. Sentence after sentence from the Desert, the "trackless place" of Antony's desire,[26] fall on the ear with a dangerous enchantment: the remoteness of death is in the lovely rhythms of the old hermit's questioning. "Tell me, I pray thee, how fares the human race: if new roofs be risen in the ancient cities: whose empire is it that now sways the world?"[27] Arsenius came from Theodosius' court and the guardianship of the young princes to Scete, hungry for a quiet that could not be shaken even by the rustling of reeds or the voice of a bird.[28] It is the same hunger that gives a sudden eloquence to a quiet aged monk whom Cassian and his friend Germanus found sitting in a crowded monastery, a monk that had been a famous solitary in the desert. The young men asked him how it came that he had left the higher life for the lower: and the whole vanished sweetness of the life of quiet is in the old man's reply. He told them of the first days in the desert when few found their way there: "the sparseness of those who at that time dwelt in the desert was gracious to us as a caress; it lavished liberty upon us, in the far-flowing vastness of that solitude." But others came to know the sweetness of the quiet which their coming destroyed: *coangus-*

tata vastiori eremi libertate (no English word can give the poignancy of the Latin *angustus*); the vaster freedom of the desert was cabined, and the fire of divine contemplation grew cold. Sublimity was gone: let him make up for it by obedience. So the old man came back from the desert, now a thoroughfare, to submit to the yoke of his abbot's will and the friction of living among men.[29]

The truth is that solitude is the creative condition of genius, religious or secular, and the ultimate sterilising of it. No human soul can for long ignore "the giant agony of the world" and live, except indeed the mollusc life, a barnacle upon eternity. No artist ever desired the soundless world more fervently than the younger Keats: it is as though he foresaw the baptism where-with he was to be baptised, and shuddered from it. *Lear* haunted him: "Do you not hear the sea?" The black moods in which "Po-etry, Ambition and Love" passed by him with averted face, when the creation of beauty seemed to him an impertinence in the face of anguish, and a poet's coronation an outrage in a world "where women have cancers," these are barren for the craftsman, but the matrix of the supreme artist. The second ver-sion of *Hyperion* is lamentable, but the sickness that ailed it was "an immortal sickness which kills not: it works a constant change," till it brought him to

> "The moving waters at their priestlike task
> Of pure ablution round earth's human shores,"

where every word is an abyss of human experience.

The Desert itself came to realize that solitude is a thing to be earned; and the Venerable Bede's account of St. Cuthbert's de-parture from Lindisfarne is the consummation of its wisdom.

To Cuthbert, the solitude of Farne island "sieged on this side and on that by the deep and infinite sea," was the reward of a lifetime of journeying and preaching among the Border fells, and endurance of that community life, which can be, said the Buddha, like swordgrass in one's hand. "So in that same monastery he fulfilled many years; and at last, with the goodwill of his abbot and brethren to company him, he set out in deep delight towards that secret solitude for which he had so long desired and sought and striven. The coming and going of the active life had done its long work upon him, and he rejoiced that now he had earned his right to climb to the quiet mediation upon God."[30] The abbot Longinus said to the abbot Lucius that he was minded to shut himself into his cell and refuse the face of men, that he might perfect himself: "Unless thou first amend thy life going to and fro amongst men," said the abbot Lucius, "thou shall not avail to amend it dwelling alone." "If thou seest a young man ascending up to heaven by his own will, catch him by the foot and throw him down, for it is not expedient for him."[31] That saying is ascribed vaguely to "certain of the Fathers," but it savours of the ruggedness of Macarius, who could be gentler with a blinded hyena-kitten,[32] than with his own kind. Yet for two young men, his heart was soft enough. Rufinus told the story, and put style on it:[33] the abbot Vindemius also told it, and was wise enough to give it word for word as he had heard it from the saint himself. It is worth transcribing in full, for it is a summary of the Desert initiation.

"The abbot Vindemius used to tell how Macarius told him this story, saying, 'Once when I was living in Scete, there came down two youths, strangers. One of them was beginning to grow a beard, the other not yet. They came to me asking, "Where is the cell of the abbot Macarius?" And I said, "What is your will with him?" They made answer, "We have heard of him, and are come to Scete to see him." I say to them, "I am he." They asked my pardon and said, "Here we would like to abide." But I, seeing them delicate and seemingly come of wealthy folk, said to them, "Ye cannot stay here." He that was the elder said, "If we cannot stay here, we shall look for some other place." Then I said within my heart, "Why should I harry them, and they be offended?" The very hardship will make them flee of themselves." And I said to them, "Come, make yourselves a cell, if ye can." And they said, "Only show us how, and we shall do it." So I gave them an axe, and a basket of loaves, and salt: and I showed them a hard rock and said, "Quarry this, and bring yourselves logs from the marsh: and when ye have put on the roof, abide in the one place": but I was thinking that because of the hard toil they would flee. But they questioned me, saying, "What shall we work on, here?" I say to them, "Plaiting palm-leaves," and taking leaves from the palm-trees in the marsh, I showed them the beginning of a plait, and how to join them together. And I said to them, "Make baskets, and give them to the sacristans at the church, and they will supply you with bread." After this I went away from them; but they patiently carried out everything I told them, and they did not come to me for three years. And I waited, debating in my heart, saying to myself, "How, think you, do they do, that they have never come to ask counsel of me about their thoughts? Some that are a great way off come to me, but these that are close to me come not: nor have they gone to any other, unless only to church to receive in silence the Host." So I prayed to God fasting for a week, that He would show me how they did. And when the week was ended, I rose up and went to see them, how they lived. And when I knocked, they opened to me and greeted me in silence, and I prayed and sat down. The elder nodded to the younger to go out, and himself sat weaving a plait, speaking not at all. And towards the ninth hour, he made a sign by knocking, and the younger came in and made a little stew of vegetables. And at the elder's nod, he brought a table and set three farls on it and stood silent. But I said, "Rise, let us eat": and we rose and ate: and he brought a little jar, and we drank. And when evening was come, they said to me, "Dost thou go away?" I answered, "Nay, I shall sleep here." So they laid a mat for me in one place, and for themselves in another corner apart: and they took off their girdles and their aprons and together laid themselves down on their mat to sleep, before me. And when they had lain down, I prayed to God, that He would show me the manner of their toil. And the roof of their cell was opened, and there shone a great light as of day: but they themselves saw it not. But when they thought that I was asleep, the elder touched the younger on the side. And they rose up and girdled themselves, and stood in silence, stretching out their hands to heaven. And I saw them, but they did not see me. And I saw evil spirits like flies coming about the younger brother and some even coming to sit on his mouth, some on his eyes. And I saw an angel of God with a sword of fire going like a rampart round about him and fighting the demons from him. But they could not come near the elder. Towards morning they laid themselves down, and I made as though I were waking from sleep, and they did likewise. But the elder said to me this word only: "Wilt thou that we sing the XII Psalms?" I said, "Yea." And the younger brother chanted five psalms, six verses at a time, and an alleluia: and with every word there came from his mouth a torch of flame, and ascended to heaven. In like fashion when the elder opened his mouth to chant, as it were the smoke of fire rose from his mouth and reached up to heaven. And I said from my heart the office, as did they. Going out, I said, "Pray for me." And they in silence assured me. And I knew that the elder was made perfect: but that the Enemy still besieged the younger. And after a few days the elder brother slept in peace: and on the third day thereafter the younger.'

"And when other of the Fathers would come to see the abbot Macarius, he would take them into their cell, saying, 'Come see the place of martyrdom of these lesser pilgrims.'"[34]

There is something in that story of the living voice: it is as though Vindemius himself had been so moved that he kept the very intonation, the gruffness, the quick change of tense of the teller. But it is the rare word "martyrdom" that betrays the old man's humanity. For the ascetic and mystic, a swift translation to eternity and the passing of youth in the denial of youth, must seem great gain. Yet Macarius, inured as he was to abnegation and silence, is shaken by them: they died young. And to the less disciplined reader, the *vivo funere,* the living burial, of Rutilius' anger comes unbidden to the mind; Rutilius, and Dante, meeting Brunetto Latini on the lip of Hell.

> What chance or fate hath brought thee, to this place
> Ere thy last day? . . .
> Yonder above, I said, in the clear life,
> I lost myself in a valley, before my years were full.[35]

Now, that it should be so is perhaps the ultimate proof of the power of matter, the depth of the warfare between the spirit and the flesh. For the martyr's grave of these lesser pilgrims is not the only waste of youth in human experience. Leaving aside the annihilation of an entire generation in four years, not yet a quarter of a century ago, how many have died or been maimed in chemical and biological research: how many litter the track to the Northern or Southern Pole: how many have been taken by

Everest and his peers: how many dead and still to die in the conquest of the air, or in that last exploration which gives this generation its nearest approach to religious ecstasy, the annihilation
of space in speed? Gauguin, like any Desert fanatic, left his Paris
banking house and his comfortable wife, and watched his small
son starve and himself died in nakedness and ecstasy, because he
had discovered paint as the Desert discovered God. Van Gogh
went mad in struggling to paint light: they found a fragment of
a letter in his pocket after he had shot himself. "Well, my own
work, I am risking my life for it, and my reason has half
foundered in it—that's all right." It is not that these are not
grieved for: but they are not grudged. No generous spirit will
shirk the arduous, provided it be unknown. A man must follow
his star. We do not grudge it that these should have left wife and
children and lands and reason for the flick of a needle on the
speedometer or "a still life of a pair of old shoes." The only field
of research in which a man may make no sacrifices, under pain
of being called a fanatic, is God.

Yet it is legitimate to ask what harvest human thought has
reaped from the Desert fields. At first sight, it is meagre enough.
If one excepts the great names of those who came to school to the
Desert and returned from it to the more conventional life of
mankind, Basil, Chrysostom, Athanasius, Jerome, their contribution to the philosophy of religion is negligible. The richness of
the records is in their kindness, their selflessness, their humbleness: but the records are of their ways with men. There is little
or nothing of their ways with God. There is hardly a phrase in
the vast bulk of the *Vitae Patrum* that has a tithe of Augustine's
flaming power, the overmastering conviction of God that wrests
and shatters language in the letters of St. Paul: yet both these
were men burdened with world affairs, living passionate and
turbulent lives. The chapter on "Contemplation" in the *Verba*

Seniorum is the dullest and least rewarding: following as it does page after page of Socratic wisdom and humanity, it comes as an anticlimax, a patchwork of minor prophecies, commonplace materialisations of angelic and demoniac powers. Augustine's single sentence, *"Mens mea pervenit ad id quod est in ictu trepidantis aspectus"*[36] ("My mind reached that which is in the thrust of a quivering glance"), is worth a bale of it. In Cassian's *Collationes,* based on the long talks he had with the old men of the desert, sitting at their feet on a little stool of reeds, he has built up a lodge for the devout soul, line upon line, clay and bark and twig, patient and wise as a beaver: but there is little of the *arduus furor.* He has moments of rare and high eloquence, as on the ultimate reach of prayer "beyond sound of voice or movement of the tongue or any uttered word, when the mind is narrowed by no human speech, but . . . all its senses gathered in one round, leaps like a fountain toward God, discovering in one brief particle of time such things as cannot easily be spoken, nor can the mind traverse again when it comes back upon itself": and again, on the goal and consummation of prayer: "when all love, all longing, all desire, all seeking, all thoughts of ours, all that we see, all that we say, all that we hope, shall be God." But the bulk of the book is humane and gentle precept, a case book of spiritual direction, ironic and wise, as when he notes how a man who has despised wealth and pomp and great estate can be stirred to passion over a knife or a pen, and will so cling to a single codex that no man may so much as handle it: and how a devout soul intent on the peace of contemplation can break in wrath upon an interrupting brother.[37] Benedict and Dominic alike came again and again to these quiet springs and Thomas Aquinas would read a page or two of Cassian, when speculative divinity became too subtle, and the fire of love grew cold.[38]

The truth is that to look for the secret of the Desert under any form of words is to lose one's pains. They are seldom eloquent: but like the brother whose sole possession was a single codex of the gospels and who sold it to feed the hungry, and when challenged said, "I have but sold that word which ever said to me, Sell that thou hast and give to the poor," their every gesture is pregnant. This same barren chapter on "Contemplation" begins with a story that might warn the curious reader of what he will not find. "A brother went to the cell of the abbot Arsenius and looked through the window and saw the old man as it were one flame: for he was a brother worthy to look upon such things. And after he had knocked, the old man came out, and saw the brother in a maze, and said, to him, 'Hast thou been knocking long? Didst thou see aught?' And he answered him, 'Nay.' And he talked with him a while, and sent him away."[39] Again, at one time Zachary went to his master, Silvanus, and found him in a trance, his hands held up to heaven: and he closed the door and went away. He came back at the sixth hour, and again at the ninth, and still he had not moved. An hour later he came again and knocked and went in: the old man was lying still. And the young man said, "What came on thee, today, my Father?" And the old man said, "I was not well, my son." Then the young man took him by the feet and conjured him to tell him what he had seen, and the old man forced to speak replied, "I was caught up into heaven and I saw the glory of God: and I stood there until but now, and now was sent away."[40] The same Zachary on his own death-bed ("I have never yet," said his abbot, "come to the stature of his humility and his silence"), was asked by the abbot Moses, "What seest thou, my son?" And he made answer, "Naught better, Father, than to hold one's peace."[41] The Fathers talked but little of the "wingy mysteries of divinity." A famous anchorite came to take counsel on high things with the abbot Pastor, but the old man turned away his head, and the anchorite went away aggrieved. His disciple asked Pastor why he had refused to talk with a man so great and of such reputation in his own country, and the old man said that his visitor could speak of heavenly things, but that himself was of earth. "If he had spoken to me of the passions of the soul I could have answered him: but of the things of the spirit I am ignorant." And the anchorite, hearing it, had heart-searchings, and came back to the old man and said, "What shall I do, my father, for the passions of the soul have dominion over me?" And they talked a long while, and the anchorite said, "Verily, this is love's road."[42] A young man said to Sisois, "I know this of myself, that my mind is intent upon God," and the old man said to him, "It is no great matter that thy mind should be with God: but if thou didst see thyself less than any of His creatures, that were something."[43] Of the depth of their spiritual experience they had little to say: but their every action showed a standard of values that turns the world upside down. It was their humility, their gentleness, their heartbreaking courtesy that was the seal of their sanctity to their contemporaries, far beyond abstinence or miracle or sign. St. Antony himself was once questioning the brethren on the meaning of some phrase in Holy Writ, and each said what he could, but when it came to the abbot Joseph, the old man answered that he did not know. And the abbot Antony said, "Verily the abbot Joseph alone hath found the road, who saith that he doth not know."[44] There is a great gulf between the stone-quarried wisdom of the Desert and John Scotus Erigena's vision of "the light inaccessible . . . restoring and recalling to unity ineffable the seen and the unseen, the world of sense and the world of thought,"[45] but the Fathers would have joined with him in his final prayer for the coming of the light "that shall bring to darkness the false light of the philosophers, and shall lighten the darkness of those that know."[46]

Yet one intellectual concept they did give to Europe: eternity. Here again they do not formulate it: they embody it. These men, by the very exaggeration of their lives, stamped infinity on the imagination of the West. They saw the life of the body as Paulinus saw it, *"occidui temporis umbra,"* a shadow at sunset. "The spaces of our human life set over against eternity"—it is the undercurrent of all Antony's thought—"are most brief and poor."[47]

> "Think you the bargain's hard, to have exchanged
> The transient for the eternal, to have sold
> Earth to buy heaven?"[48]

Twelve centuries later, Donne could pray to be delivered from thinking

> "that this earth
> Is only for our prison fram'd,
> Or that Thou'rt covetous
> To them whom Thou lovest, or that they are maim'd
> From reaching this world's sweet who seek Thee thus."

It is the rich compromise of seventeenth-century humanism. But for the fourth century the Kingdom of God was still the pearl of great price hidden in a field, for which a man must sell all that he had if he would buy that field. Paganism was daylight, Augustine's "queen light," sovereign of the sense, rich in its acceptance of the daylight earth: but Christianity came first to the world as a starlit darkness, into which a man steps and comes suddenly aware of a whole universe, except that part of it which is beneath his feet.

"If Light can thus conceal, wherefore not Life?"

Experience was to bring compromise, the alternation of day and night, the *vita mixta* of action and contemplation, "wherein," says Augustine, "the love of truth doth ask a a holy quiet, and the necessity of love doth accept a righteous busyness."[49] But the Desert Fathers knew no compromise. They have no place among the doctors: they have no great place among even the obscurer saints. But the extravagance of their lives is the extravagance of poetry.

> "*. . . nel mondo ad ora ad ora*
> *m'insegnavate come l'uom s'eterna:*"[50]

in the world, hour by hour, they taught us how man makes himself eternal. Starved and scurvy-ridden as the first voyagers across the Atlantic, these finished with bright day and chose the dark.

And, paradoxical as it seems, their denial of the life of earth has been the incalculable enriching of it, and they have affected the consciousness of generations to which they are not even a name. They thought to devaluate time by setting it over against eternity, and instead they have given it an unplumbed depth. It is as though they first conceived of eternity as everlastingness, the production to infinity of a straight line, and in time men came to know it vertical as well as horizontal, and to judge an experience by its quality rather than its duration. The sense of infinity is now in our blood: and even to those of us who see our life as a span long, beginning in the womb and ending in the coffin or a shovelful of grey ash, each moment of it has its eternal freight.

Un punto solo m'è maggior letargo—

One point of time hath deeper burdened me
Than all the centuries that have forgot
How Argo's shadow startled first the sea.[51]

The *saecula sine fine ad requiescendum,* "the ages of quiet without end," have been transformed into Boethius' definition of eternity, "that which encloseth and possesseth the whole fullness of the life everlasting, from which naught of the future is absent, and naught of the past hath flowed away."[52] Not one of the Desert Fathers could have conceived it: they might even have denied it as a heresy: yet the mind of man moved a stage nearer to it with each moment of their ravaged lives.

THE LIFE OF ST. PAUL THE FIRST HERMIT

by St. Jerome

There is a variant reading in some of the manuscripts which suggests that the *Vita S. Pauli* was written during Jerome's own years in the desert, before he found his vocation. He had had his boyhood in Dalmatia, his learning and a young man's pleasures and the beginning of his book-collecting in Rome: had gone a scholar's journey to Trèves, copying manuscripts: made some of the friendships of his life at Aquileia: and finally broke away to wander in what he called "an uncertain pilgrimage" through Greece and Anatolia. The blazing heat in Cilicia struck him down, and he headed through Syria to find "safe harbour for my wreck" in Antioch, where his friend Evagrius seems to have preceded him. For Evagrius, the journey from Italy was a homecoming, for he had great wealth and a country house at Maronia, about twenty-eight miles south of Antioch: for Jerome, it was the first stage of the pilgrimage that was literally to end in the coming of the fourth of the Wise Men to Bethlehem, with his ambiguous gifts of exquisite scholarship and a bitter tongue. Meantime he was not yet thirty, and passionate for Cicero: the country house at Maronia was agreeable, Evagrius a generous patron, there was always someone at hand to copy a manuscript, and there were three friends, Innocent, Hylas, Heliodorus, as delightful as their names. But the Desert was too near the Town for the peace of mind of a sensitive young man. Malchus, innocent and old, was to be seen at church every day, with his epic years of desert sanctity behind him: Theodosius of Rhossus, a hermit so austere and so kind that the sailors on those coasts abandoned their familiar deities in any serious peril to cry on Theodosius' God, was a dangerous correspondent: Evagrius himself was either working on or had already finished his translation of the life of St. Antony, in itself enough to kindle a passion for the absolute that not even Cicero's suavity could assuage. And then Innocent died, and after him Hylas. By 375 Jerome was solitary in the desert of Chalcis: and what he suffered there he told years after to his girl-pupil Eustocium, with the regret of appeased middle age for the exaltation and misery of youth.[1]

"Oh, how many times did I, set in the desert, in that vast solitude parched with the fires of the sun that offers a dread abiding to the monk, how often did I think myself back in the old Roman enchantments. There I sat solitary, full of bitterness; my disfigured limbs shuddered away from the sackcloth, my dirty skin was taking on the hue of the Ethiopian's flesh: every day tears, every day sighing: and if in spite of my struggles sleep would tower over and sink upon me, my battered body ached on the naked earth. Of food and drink I say nothing, since even a sick monk uses only cold water, and to take anything cooked is wanton luxury. Yet that same I, who for fear of hell condemned myself to such a prison, I, the comrade of scorpions and wild beasts, was there, watching the maidens in their dances: my face haggard with fasting, my mind burnt with desire in my frigid body, and the fires of lust alone leaped before a man prematurely dead. So, destitute of all aid, I used to lie at the feet of Christ, watering them with my tears, wiping them with my hair, struggling to subdue my rebellious flesh with seven days' fasting. I do not blush to confess the misery of my hapless days: rather could I weep that I am not what I was once. I remember crying out till day became one with night, nor ceasing to beat my breast until my Lord would chide and tranquillity return. I grew to dread even my cell, with its knowledge of my imaginings: and grim and angry with myself, would set out solitary to explore the desert: and wherever I would spy the depth of a valley or a mountainside or a precipitous rock, there was my place of prayer, there the torture-house of my unhappy flesh: and, the Lord Himself is witness, after many tears, and eyes that clung to heaven, I would sometimes seem to myself to be one with the angelic hosts."[2]

He left the Desert after five years: and though he was afterwards to cry, "Then the desert held me: would that it had never let me go!"[3] it is to be remembered that Jerome was a Virgilian romantic. Even in this *Life of the First Hermit,* Antony, who distrusted literature, is tripped up by a quotation from the *Æneid* at every step. "I toiled hard," said Jerome ruefully, "to deject my style: but however it comes, you may fill a jar with water and it still will smell of the wine that steeped it first."[4] For Jerome's books went with him to the desert. "For many a year had I cut myself off from home and parents and sister and kin and what is harder than these, the habit of exquisite dining . . . but the library I had built up with such ardour and pains in Rome, I could not bring myself to do without."[5] The solitude of the desert drove him, not to silence, but to the mastering of another language. No fasting could tame the intolerable energy of his imagination. He must have something craggy to break his mind upon: and he found it in Hebrew. "When I was a young man," he wrote to his friend Rusticus, "and the solitude of the desert walled me in, I could not endure the stinging of my lusts, the heat of my nature. The flesh I might try to break with frequent fasting: but my mind was seething with imagination: so to tame it, I gave myself up for training to one of the brethren, a Hebrew who had come to the faith: and so, after the subtlety of Quintilian, the flowing river of Cicero, the gravity of Fronto and the gentleness of Pliny, I began to learn another alphabet, and meditate on words that hissed and words that gasped. What toil I spent, what difficulty I endured, how many times despaired and threw it up, how many times contentiously returned to begin anew, my own conscience is witness that endured it, and those that lived their life beside me: and I thank God that out of that bitter seed of letters I plucked so sweet a fruit."[6] Christendom had still more reason to thank God: the final vintage was to be the Vulgate translation of the Old Testament: he was still working on Hebrew in his old age.

Meantime, however, the sufferings of an Italianate body in the Syrian desert combined with the internecine warfare of the three bishops of Antioch over the three Hypostases of the Trinity to drive him back, first to Constantinople, and then to the adamant security of St. Peter's see, and the familiar lyrical enchantment of Rome.[7] The wise Pope Damasus had divined where his genius lay, and set him to his master-work of translation, first from the Greek: recension after recension, and the rich amenities of scholarly controversy, were to keep him happy till he died. But when he made the bibliography of his own books for his catalogue of Illustrious Men, the *Vita S. Pauli* came first in the list:[8] and when after a long silence he began to write again in Bethlehem, it was the story of Malchus of the Desert that he had heard from him a lifetime before, in the good days at Maronia. "This is the story Malchus, that was an old man, told to me that was a young one: and this I tell you, now that I am old. . . . And do ye tell it to those that come after you, how amid swords and deserts and wild beasts, chastity never was captive:

and how a man devoted to Christ may die, but cannot be defeated."[9]

THE LIFE OF ST. PAUL THE FIRST HERMIT
Prologue

There is a good deal of uncertainty abroad as to which monk it was who first came to live in the desert. Some, questing back to a remoter age, would trace the beginning from the Blessed Elias and from John: yet of these Elias seems to us to have been rather a prophet than a monk: and John to have begun to prophesy before ever he was born. Some on the other hand (and these have the crowd with them) insist that Antony was the founder of this way of living, which in one sense is true: not so much that he was before all others, as that it was by him their passion was wakened. Yet Amathas, who buried the body of his master, and Macarius, both of them Antony's disciples, now affirm that a certain Paul of Thebes was the first to enter on the road. This is my own judgment, not so much from the facts as from conviction. Some tattle this and that, as the fancy takes them, a man in an underground cavern with hair to his heels; and the like fantastic inventions which it were idle to track down. A lie that is impudent needs no refuting.

So then, since there is a full tradition as regards Antony, both in the Greek and Roman tongues, I have determined to write a little of Paul's beginning and his end; rather because the story has been passed over, than confident of any talent of mine. But what was his manner of life in middle age, or what wiles of Satan he resisted, has been discovered to none of mankind.

The Life

During the reign of Decius and Valerian, the persecutors, about the time when Cornelius at Rome, Cyprian at Carthage, spilt their glorious blood, a fierce tempest made havoc of many churches in Egypt and Thebaid. It was the Christian's prayer in those days that he might, for Christ's sake, die by the sword. But their crafty enemy sought out torments wherein death came slowly: desiring rather to slaughter the soul than the body. And as Cyprian wrote, who was himself to suffer: *They long for death, and dying is denied them.* . . .

Now at this very time, while such deeds as these were being done, the death of both parents left Paul heir to great wealth in the Lower Thebaid: his sister was already married. He was then about fifteen years of age, excellently versed alike in Greek and Egyptian letters, of a gentle spirit, and a strong lover of God. When the storm of persecution began its thunder, he betook himself to a farm in the country, for the sake of its remoteness and secrecy. But

> "*What wilt thou not drive mortal hearts to do,*
> *O thou dread thirst for gold?*"

His sister's husband began to meditate the betrayal of the lad whom it was his duty to conceal. Neither the tears of his wife, nor the bond of blood, nor God looking down upon it all from on high, could call him back from the crime, spurred on by a cruelty that seemed to ape religion. The boy, far-sighted as he was, had the wit to discern it, and took flight to the mountains, there to wait while the persecution ran its course. What had been his necessity became his free choice. Little by little he made his way, sometimes turning back and again returning, till at length he came upon a rocky mountain, and at its foot, at no great distance, a huge cave, its mouth closed by a stone. There is a thirst in men to pry into the unknown: he moved the stone, and eagerly exploring came within on a spacious courtyard open to the sky, roofed by the wide-spreading branches of an ancient palm, and with a spring of clear shining water: a stream ran hasting from it and was soon drunk again, through a narrow opening, by the same earth that had given its waters birth. There were, moreover, not a few dwelling-places in that hollow mountain, where one might see chisels and anvils and hammers for the minting of coin. Egyptian records declare that the place was a mint for coining false money, at the time that Antony was joined to Cleopatra.

So then, in this beloved habitation, offered to him as it were by God himself, he lived his life through in prayer ad solitude: the palm-tree provided him with food and clothing. And lest this should seem impossible to any, I call Jesus to witness and His holy angels, that I myself, in that part of the desert which marches with Syria and the Saracens, have seen monks, one of whom lived a recluse for thirty years, on barley bread and muddy water: another in an ancient well (which in the heathen speech of Syria is called a *quba*) kept himself in life on five dry figs a day. These things will seem incredible to those who believe not that all things are possible to him that believeth.

But to return to that place from which I have wandered; for a hundred and thirteen years the Blessed Paul lived the life of heaven upon earth, while in another part of the desert Antony abode, an old man of ninety years. And as Antony himself would tell, there came suddenly into his mind the thought that no better monk than he had his dwelling in the desert. But as he lay quiet that night it was revealed to him that there was deep in the desert another better by far than he, and that he must make haste to visit him. And straightway as day was breaking the venerable old man set out, supporting his feeble limbs on his staff, to go he knew not whither. And now came burning noon, the scorching sun overhead, yet would he not flinch from the journey begun, saying, "I believe in my God that He will shew me His servant as He said." Hardly had he spoken when he espied a man that was part horse, whom the imagination of the poets has called the Hippocentaur. At sight of him, the saint did arm his forehead with the holy sign. "How there," said he, "in what part of the country hath this servant of God his abode?" The creature gnashed out some kind of barbarous speech, and rather grinding his words than speaking them, sought with his bristling jaws to utter as gentle discourse as might be: holding out his right hand he pointed out the way, and so made swiftly off across the open plains and vanished from the saint's wondering eyes. And indeed whether the devil had assumed this shape to terrify him, or whether (as might well be) the desert that breeds monstrous beasts begat this creature also, we have no certain knowledge.

So then Antony, in great amaze and turning over in his mind that thing that he had seen, continued on his way. Nor was it long till in a rocky alley he saw a dwarfish figure of no great size, its nostrils joined together, and its forehead bristling with horns: the lower part of its body ended in goat's feet. Unshaken by the sight, Antony, like a good soldier, caught up the shield of faith and the buckler of hope. The creature thus described, however, made to offer him dates as tokens of peace: and perceiving this, Antony hastened his step, and asking him who he might be, had this reply: "Mortal am I, and one of the dwellers in the desert, whom the heathen worship, astray in diverse error, calling us Fauns, and Satyrs, and Incubi. I come on an embassy from my tribe. We pray thee that thou wouldst entreat for us our common God who did come, we know, for the world's salvation, and His sound hath gone forth over all the earth." Hearing him speak thus, the old wayfarer let his tears run down, tears that sprang from the mighty joy that was in his heart. For he rejoiced for Christ's glory and the fall of Satan: marvelling that he could understand his discourse, and striking the ground with his staff, "Woe to thee, Alexandria," he cried, "who dost worship monsters in room of God. Woe to thee, harlot city, in whom the demons of all the earth have flowed together. What hast thou now to say? The beasts speak Christ and thou dost worship monsters in room of God." He had not yet left speaking, when the frisky creature made off as if on wings. And this, lest any hesitation should stir in the incredulous, is maintained by universal witness during the reign of Constantius. For a man of this type was brought alive to Alexandria, and was made a great show for the people: and his lifeless corpse was thereafter preserved with salt, lest it should disintegrate in the heat of summer, and brought to Antioch, to be seen by the Emperor.

But to return to my purpose: Antony continued to travel through the region he had entered upon, now gazing at the tracks of wild beasts, and now at the vastness of the broad desert: what he should do, whither he should turn, he knew not. The second day had ebbed to its close: one still remained, if he were not to think that Christ had left him. All night long he spent the darkness in prayer, and in the doubtful light of dawn he saw a she-wolf, panting in a frenzy of thirst, steal into the foot of the mountain. He followed her with his eyes, and coming up to the cave into which she had disappeared, began to peer within; but his curiosity availed him nothing, the darkness repelled his sight. Yet perfect love, as the Scripture saith, casteth out fear: holding his breath and stepping cautiously the wary explorer went in.

Advancing little by little, and often standing still, his ear caught a sound. Afar off, in the dread blindness of the dark he saw a light; hurrying too eagerly, he struck his foot against a stone, and raised a din. At the sound the Blessed Paul shut the door which had been open, and bolted it. Then did Antony fall upon the ground outside the door, and there he prayed for admittance until the sixth hour and beyond it. "Who I am," said he, "and whence, and why I have come, thou knowest. I know that I am not worthy to behold thee: nevertheless, unless I see thee, I go not hence. Thou who receivest beasts, why dost thou turn away men? I have sought, and I have found: I knock, that it may be opened to me. But if I prevail not, here shall I die before thy door. Assuredly thou wilt bury my corpse."

And so he stood, pleading, and fixed there,
To him the hero answered, in few words:

"No man pleads thus, who comes to threaten: no man comes to injure, who comes in tears: and dost thou marvel that I receive thee not, if it is a dying man that comes?" And so jesting, Paul set open the door. And the two embraced each other and greeted one another by their names, and together returned thanks to God. And after the holy kiss, Paul sat down beside Antony, and began to speak. "Behold him whom thou hast sought with so much labour, a shaggy white head and limbs worn out with age. Behold, thou lookest on a man that is soon to be dust. Yet because love endureth all things tell me, I pray thee, how fares the human race: if new roofs be risen in the ancient cities, whose empire is it that now sways the world; and if any still survive, snared in the error of the demons."

And as they talked they perceived that a crow had settled on a branch of the tree, and softly flying down, deposited a whole loaf before their wondering eyes. And when he had withdrawn, "Behold," said Paul, "God hath sent us our dinner, God the merciful, God the compassionate. It is now sixty years since I have had each day a half loaf of bread: but at thy coming, Christ hath doubled His soldiers' rations." And when they had given thanks to God, they sat down beside the margin of the crystal spring. But now sprang up a contention between them as to who should break the bread, that brought the day wellnigh to evening, Paul insisting on the right of the guest, Antony countering by right of seniority. At length they agreed that each should take hold of the loaf and pull toward himself, and let each take what remained in his hands. Then they drank a little water, holding their mouths to the spring: and offering to God the sacrifice of praise, they passed the night in vigil.

But as day returned to the earth, the Blessed Paul spoke to Antony. "From old time, my brother, I have known that thou wert a dweller in these parts: from old time God had promised that thou, my fellow-servant, wouldst come to me. But since the time has come for sleeping, and (for I have ever desired to be dissolved and to be with Christ) the race is run, there remaineth for me a crown of righteousness; thou hast been sent by God to shelter this poor body in the ground, returning earth to earth."

At this Antony, weeping and groaning, began pleading with him not to leave him but take him with him as a fellow-traveller on that journey.

"Thou must not," said the other, "seek thine own, but another's good. It were good for thee, the burden of the flesh flung down, to follow the Lamb: but it is good for the other brethren that they should have thine example for their grounding. Wherefore, I pray thee, unless it be too great a trouble, go and bring the cloak which Athanasius the Bishop gave thee, to wrap around my body." This indeed the Blessed Paul asked, not because he much cared whether his dead body should rot covered or naked, for indeed he had been clothed for so long time in woven palm-leaves: but he would have Antony far from him, that he might spare him the pain of his dying.

Then Antony, amazed that Paul should have known of Athanasius and the cloak, dared make no answer: it seemed to him that he saw Christ in Paul, and he worshipped God in Paul's heart: silently weeping, he kissed his eyes and his hands, and set out on the return journey to the monastery, the same which in aftertime was captured by the Saracens. His steps indeed could not keep pace with his spirit: yet though length of days had broken a body worn out with fasting, his mind triumphed over his years. Exhausted and panting, he reached his dwelling, the journey ended. Two disciples who of long time had ministered to him, ran to meet him, saying, "Where hast thou so long tarried, Master?"

"Woe is me," he made answer, "that do falsely bear the name of monk. I have seen Elias, I have see John in the desert, yea, I have seen Paul in paradise." And so, with tight-pressed lips and his hand beating his breast, he carried the cloak from his cell. To his disciples eager to know more of what was toward, he answered, "There is a time to speak, and there is a time to be silent." And leaving the house, and not even taking some small provision for the journey, he again took the road by which he had come: athirst for him, longing for the sight of him, eyes and mind intent. For he feared as indeed befell, that in his absence, Paul might have rendered back to Christ the spirit that he owed Him.

And now the second day dawned upon him, and for three hours he had been on the way, when he saw amid a host of angels and amid the companies of prophets and apostles, Paul climbing the steeps of heaven, and shining white as snow. And straightway falling on his face he threw sand upon his head and wept saying, "Paul, why didst thou send me away? Why dost thou go with no leavetaking? So tardy to be known, art thou so swift to go?"

In aftertime the Blessed Antony would tell how speedily he covered the rest of the road, as it might be a bird flying. Nor was it without cause. Entering the cave, he saw on its bent knees, the head erect and the hands stretched out to heaven, the lifeless body: yet first, thinking he yet lived, he knelt and prayed beside him. Yet no accustomed sigh of prayer came to him: he kissed him, weeping, and then knew that the dead body of the holy man still knelt and prayed to God, to whom all things live.

So then he wrapped the body round and carried it outside, chanting the hymns and psalms of Christian tradition. But sadness came on Antony, because he had no spade to dig the ground. His mind was shaken, turning this way and that. "For if I should go back to the monastery," he said, "it is a three days' journey: if I stay here, there is no more that I can do. Let me die, therefore, as is meet: and falling beside thy soldier, Christ, let me draw my last breath."

But even as he pondered, behold two lions came coursing, their manes flying, from the inner desert, and made towards him. At sight of them, he was at first in dread: then, turning his mind to God, he waited undismayed, as though he looked on doves. They came straight to the body of the holy dead, and halted by it wagging their tails, then couched themselves at his feet, roaring mightily; and Antony well knew they were lamenting him, as best they could. Then, going a little way off, they began to scratch up the ground with their paws, vying with one another in throwing up the sand, till they had dug a grave roomy enough for a man: and thereupon, as though to ask the reward of their work, they came up to Antony, with drooping ears and downbent heads, licking his hands and his feet. He saw that they were begging for his blessing; and pouring out his soul in praise to Christ for that even the dumb beasts feel that there is God, "Lord," he said, "without whom no leaf lights from the tree, nor a single sparrow falls upon the ground, give unto these even as Thou knowest."

Then, motioning with his hand, he signed to them to depart. And when they had gone away, he bowed his aged shoulders under the weight of the holy body: and laying it in the grave, he gathered the earth above it, and made the wonted mound. Another day broke: and then, lest the pious heir should receive none of the goods of the intestate, he claimed for himself the tunic which the saint had woven out of palm-leaves as one weaves baskets. And so returning to the monastery, he told the whole story to his disciples in order as it befell: and on the solemn feasts of Easter and Pentecost, he wore the tunic of Paul.

. . . I pray you, whoever ye be who read this, that ye be mindful of Jerome the sinner: who, if the Lord gave him his choice, would rather have the tunic of Paul with his merits, than the purple of Kings with their thrones.

HISTORY OF THE MONKS
OF EGYPT

translated from the Greek by Rufinus of Aquileia

To Jerome at Maronia, still hesitating on the brink of renunciation, there came the news that Rufinus of Aquileia was come from over sea: that he was in Egypt, a pilgrim to the holy places: that he was in Nitria: that he had seen Macarius. After that, nothing but fever kept Jerome in his bed. "Never," he wrote to his friend, "did sailor tempest-tossed so look for harbour: never did parched field so thirst for rain: never did mother on the curving shore keep so anxious watch for her son." It has its irony, especially in the conclusion: "There is no way of buying love. Friendship that can end was never true."[1] This friendship that was famous over Christendom ended in hateful and intimate wounding and blazoned outrage. "Is there any friend," wrote Augustine, in meddlesome but sincere agitation, "is there any friend one will not dread as a future foe, when this that we bewail hath raised its head between Jerome and Rufinus ... men so closely knit in study and in friendship ... ripe in years, together in the very land Our Lord once walked with human feet?"[2]

There had been a touch of hysteria in Jerome's adulation of his friend. "Ask me not," he had written to Floentius, "to describe his virtues: you can trace in him the very footprints of saintliness: and I, vile mud and ashes, a dying spark, content if

[44]

my feeble foolish eyes can but endure the beholding of his splendour."[3] But there is no hysteria in the objurgation, when it
comes. If ever a man kept his sword like a dancer, till he used it
like an assassin, it was he. Jerome afloat on honeyed seas, his
decks "glutinous," in his own revolting phrase, with affection,[4]
the clean lines of his prose, muffled with bunting, is a very different craft from Jerome raking into action, grey and set, with a
wicked glint of steel. For the quarrel that rose between these
two had more poisoned springs than the question of the ortho-
doxy of the great Origen, the master-light of the Greek Fathers.
Their hate was an elixir of all academic hates, the theologian at
once accusing, and accused, of heresy, the translator impugned
for suppressing, or failing to suppress, obnoxious passages, the
editor of texts indignant at a false ascription, the fellow-student
betraying one's secret preferences in literature. Each wrote what
he called an Apologia, and each referred to the other's apology
as an Invective: but the line between defence and attack is noto-
riously uncertain. Undoubtedly the most grateful passages are
those in which Rufinus denounces, and Jerome admits, his in-
curable addiction to quoting from the classics. Unluckily for
Jerome, he had given solemn publicity some years before to a
dream in which he had been flogged before Christ's Judgment
seat for being a better Ciceronian than a Christian and had
sworn "If I hold or read a secular codex again, I have denied
Thee."[5] Does he ever write a page asks Rufinus, that does not
proclaim him a Ciceronian, a page without "our Tully," "our
Flaccus," "our Maro" at every turn? Is he not for ever puffing
his Chrysippus and Aristides and Empedocles like smoke into
his readers' faces, bragging about reading books of Pythagoras
that the learned say do not exist, edifying the ladies with examples, not from Holy Writ, but from his Tully, Flaccus, his Maro?
"I can call to witness any number of brethren living in my own

monastery on the Mount of Olives that made any number of copies for him of the Dialogues of Cicero: I have often had the quires in my own hands whilst they were writing: and I know that he paid a much higher fee for them than for other transcripts. Once he came from Bethlehem to Jerusalem to see me and brought a codex with him, a Dialogue of Cicero, and the same in Greek of Plato: he cannot deny that he gave it to me, and it was about the house a great while."[6] Jerome admits the charge with equanimity. Even donkeys, he says blandly, know the little turnings in a road they have travelled twice. He was well grounded in his youth: odd that Rufinus should marvel at his memory for Latin, when Rufinus himself without a master became acquainted with Greek? Then, more gravely, "Dye the wool purple, and no water will cleanse it. I must drink of the waters of Lethe if I am to be blamed for remembering the poems that once I knew." As for the dream-oath, are dreams to be admitted as evidence? The Prophets forbid, or Jerome will go to hell for adultery, and a martyr's crown will waft him to the skies. He has many a time dreamed of flying over mountains and seas: will Rufinus insist that his flanks have wings?[7] "Irony and tergiversation," roars Rufinus in an exasperated bellow, "are abomination to God."[8] He might, with that conviction, have taken the count at once.

For it is not the vigour of the knock-out that one commends in Jerome: it is the smiling ease of the approach, the sinister lightness on his toes. "Do but confess that Origen hath erred: and not one squeak [*mu*] shall you hear from me more. Say that he thought ill of the Son, worse of the Holy Ghost . . . that he professes the Resurrection in one phrase, destroys it in another: asserts that after many centuries and one grand restoration of all things, he will be Gabriel that was the Devil, and Paul, was Caiaphus once, and virgins, prostitutes." Is himself accused of a leaning towards the great heretic? "It does me small damage to have said that Origen who surpassed all men in his other works surpassed himself upon the *Song of Songs*: nor do I quake to hear that when I was a young man I pronounced him a doctor of the Church. . . . It has not been my habit," superbly and mendaciously, "to insult their errors, whose genius I marvel at."[9]

It is a painful business, as the passage at arms with Augustine is not. If Augustine is chastised, it is the chastisement of a fiery and arrogant young man, convinced that he knows Jerome's business better than Jerome's self, and eager to explain to the veteran author how he might turn his talents to better account. The old lion does but shift an indolent paw. "Thou that art a young man and secure on thy bishop's throne, do thou teach the peoples, and enrich the rooftrees of Rome with this new wealth of Africa. Enough for me in this poor corner of my monastery to whisper on, with one reader and an audience of one."[10] No man knew better than Augustine how deadly was that whisper, how universal that audience: and as for that unpardonable "new wealth of Africa," how often hereafter was it to come between him and the rich bouquet of his prose. Yet here, one's humanity is not engaged. With Augustine, Jerome is a maître d'armes; with Rufinus, a matador. The bull was formidable enough, courageous and clumsy; but one knows it doomed. Moreover, Jerome has himself to thank if he has endeared his rival to all posterity. He should not have called him Grunnius; should not have told us that he walked like a tortoise and talked in little grunts and hiccoughs; how he set his books in a row before he lectured; how he brought his eyebrows down and narrowed his nostrils, and cracked his little fingers by way of warning that a good thing was coming; how he beamed at table and paced along in a little wedge of cheerful chattering admirers, all well-dined at his expense; and having said all these things, which might pass for amicable clowning, he should not have stabbed out his "Cato without, Nero within."[11] The mask slips there; one sees the grin of hate. It is a good piece of prose, and Grunnius walks his tortoise walk in it for ever. But it would have been better for Jerome if he had never written it; for when he was writing it, he knew that Grunnius was dead.

To read the preface to Rufinus' translation of the *Historia Monachorum,* after these bitter exchanges, is to find a new poignancy in it. His original was in Greek, the story of a pilgrimage made through Egypt in 394, by a brother, possibly Timotheus, from Rufinus' own monastery on the Mount of Olives:[12] but he himself had made that journey twenty years before, and now and then he amplifies the text with the warmth of a personal memory. The kindness of the brethren on Mount Nitria and in Scete is recalled with a kind of nostalgia: and the prose of the preface itself has an extraordinary and haunting tenderness.

"I have seen among them many fathers that lived the life of heaven in the world. . . . I have seen some of them so purged of all thought or suspicion of malice that they no more remembered that evil was still wrought upon the earth. . . . They dwell dispersed throughout the desert and separate in their cells, but bound together by love. . . . Quiet are they and gentle. . . . They have indeed a great rivalry among them. . . . it is who shall be more merciful than his brother, kinder, humbler, more patient. If any be more learned than the rest, he carries himself so commonplace and ordinary towards all that he seems to be as Our Lord said the least among them and the servant of them all. . . . So because God gave me this boon, that I saw them and shared their life, I shall now try to tell of them, one by one, as God shall bring them to my mind: so that those who have not seen them in the body . . . may by the reading be drawn to imitate their holy toil, and seek the palm of perfect wisdom and of patience."[13]

Translation or no translation, Jerome had no doubts about the authorship; he was certain that Rufinus wrote it, inventing freely. "Many he described as monks, that never were; and by his account of them, Origenites damned out of all doubt by the bishops."[14] Did Rufinus, transcribing the story of the aged Benus who surpassed all men in his gentleness and rid the countryside of a certain beast that is called a Hippopotamus, reflect on the terrible little scholar in Bethlehem, busily routing himself? Palladius, visiting in Bethlehem about this time, spoke his mind freely on its most distinguished inhabitant. Jerome's command of the Roman speech was superb, he said, his genius renowned; but his malice was such that no saint could live within miles of him. There was Oxyperentius from Italy, Peter from Egypt, Simeon too, all of them men I had observed myself, said Palladius, and he got rid of them all. Palladius' own host, Possidonius, "gentle, austere, and of such innocence I never saw the like," assured him that he personally had never remembered any injury for more than half a day: but it did not prevent him from asserting on the strength of long acquaintance with the saint that Paula, the noble Roman lady who took care of him, had died before her time, freed at last from his malice.[15] This, however, was said *mihi in aurem,* only in Palladius' ear; and Palladius did not publish his reminiscences until Jerome too was dead. It would have gone near to crush a heart that was already broken, for Paula, and for Rome.

Palladius said of Rufinus that a more learned or a gentler was not found among men.[16] For Jerome, the absorbed concentration that Carpaccio caught in his *San Girolamo nel suo studio* has set his name with Scaliger's in the saints' calendar of scholarship:

he had, like Swift, a strange two-edged power of prose that could kill a heart, or break it with a sudden revelation of his own; and for his humanity, is there not the evidence of his lion and his donkey? It is true that legend stole them from Gerasimus, a gentler and less distinguished abbot further up the Jordan, but the blindworm judgment of posterity sometimes struggles towards the light, and when it gave them to the great and irascible scholar and even put in Jerome's mouth the unforgettable, "Do not nag at him, my brethren" [*Obsecro vos, fratres . . . hunc tamen ne exasperetis*],[17] it was in vision of a Jerome assuaged, a Jerome who had added to knowledge, patience, and to patience brotherly kindness, and to brotherly kindness charity.

HISTORY OF THE MONKS OF EGYPT

iv. We saw another old man that surpassed all men in his gentleness, Benus by name, of whom the brethren that lived with him declared that never had an oath or lie come from his mouth, nor had any of mankind ever seen him angry, or saying an unnecessary or idle word, but that his life went by in a great silence, and he was quiet in his ways, and in all things he lived as an angel might: moreover he was of vast humility, and in all conjuncture did reckon himself as of no account. And in the end, when we set upon him to let us hear some discourse from him to our edification, it was that we could do to persuade him: and he spoke to us a little about gentleness.

At one time, a certain beast that is called a hippopotamus was laying waste the neighbouring countryside, and the farmer folk asked him and he went to the place, and when he saw the monstrous creature he said to her, "I command thee, in the name of

Jesus Christ, lay waste this land no more." And she fled as though an Angel gave chase, and was no more seen. And a crocodile also, they declare, was put to flight by him at another time, in similar fashion.

vi. And we saw another holy man not far from the city [Oxyrinchus] at that part which goes towards the desert, one Theon by name, a hermit enclosed in his cell, who had kept the discipline of silence for thirty years: and who did so many miracles that he was esteemed among them as a prophet. For a great multitude of sick folk would come to him day after day, and he would reach out his hand through the window, and lay it on the head of each one, and bless them, and send them away whole of all their sickness. The very sight of him was so noble, and such reverence bore he in his face that he seemed an Angel among men, so joyous were his eyes and so full of all grace did he appear....

He was learned not only in the Egyptian and the Greek tongues, but in the Latin also, as we discovered from himself, and from those who were about him. Wishing to lighten and refresh us from the weariness of our pilgrimage, he wrote to us on tables, showing us the grace and wisdom of his discourse. His food was cooked on no fire. They said of him that at night he would go out to the desert, and for company a great troop of the beasts of the desert would go with him. And he would draw water from his well and offer them cups of it, in return for their kindness in attending him. One evidence of this was plain to see, for the tracks of gazelle and goat and the wild ass were thick about his cell.

xvi. We saw also the cell of the holy Paphnutius, the man of God, that was the most famous of the anchorites in these parts, and that had lived the most remote inhabitant of the desert round about Heracleos, that shining city of the Thebaid.

Of him we had a most warrantable account from the Fathers, how at one time, after living an angelic life, he had prayed to God that He would show him which of the saints he was thought to be like. And an angel stood by him and answered that he was like a certain singing man, that earned his bread by singing in the village. Dumbfounded at the strangeness of the answer, he made his way with all haste to the village, and sought for the man. And when he had found him, he questioned him closely as to what works of piety and religion he had ever done, and narrowly inquired into all his deeds. But the man answered that the truth was that he was a sinful man of degraded life, and that not long before from being a robber he had sunk to the squalid craft which he was now seen to exercise. But for this Paphnutius was the more insistent, asking if perchance some good thing might have cropped up amidst his thieving. "I can think of nothing good about me," said he: "but this I know that once when I was among the robbers we captured a virgin conse-crated to God: and when the rest of my company were for de-flowering her, I threw myself in the midst and snatched her from their staining, and brought her by night as far as the town, and restored her untouched to her house.

"Another time too I found a comely woman wandering in the desert. And when I asked her why and how she had come into these parts, 'Ask me nothing,' said she, 'nor question me for rea-sons, that am the wretchedest of women, but if it pleases thee to have a handmaid, take me where thou wilt. I have a husband that for arrears of tax hath often been hung up and scourged, and is kept in prison and tortured, nor ever brought out unless to suffer torment. We had three sons also, that were taken for the same debt. And because they seek me also to suffer the same pains, I flee in my misery from place to place, worn out with grief and hunger, and I have been in hiding, wandering through these parts, and for three days have had no food.' And when I heard this, I had pity for her, and took her to the cave and restored her soul that was faint with hunger and gave her the three hundred solidi for which she and her husband and their three sons were liable, she said, not only to slavery but to torture; and she returned to the city and paid the money and freed them all."

Then said Paphnutius, "I have done naught like that: yet I think it may have come to thine ears that the name of Paphnutius is famous among the monks. For it was with no small pains that I sought to fashion my life in this kind of discipline. Wherefore God hath shown me this concerning thee, that thou hast no less merit before Him than I. And so, brother, seeing that thou hast not the lowest room with God, neglect not thy soul." And straightway he flung away the pipes that he carried in his hand, and followed him to the desert, and transforming his skill in music into a spiritual harmony of life and mind, he gave himself for three whole years to the strictest abstinence, busying himself day and night in psalms and prayer, and taking the heavenly road with the powers of the soul, gave up his spirit amid the angelic host of the saints.

. . . And again Paphnutius entreated the Lord that He would show him his like upon the earth. And again the voice of the Lord came to him saying, "Know that thou art like the headman of the village close by." And on hearing this, Paphnutius made haste to go to him, and knocked at the door of his house. And he, whose habit it was to entertain strangers, ran to meet him and brought him into his house and bathed his feet and set a table before him and made a feast. And as they feasted, Paphnutius began to question his host as to his doings, what was his desire, and what his exercises in good living. But he spoke humbly of himself, liking better to hide in his good deeds than be made a talk of, and Paphnutius urged him, saying that it had been revealed to him by the Lord that he was worthy of the monastic fellowship. But at that he thought still more humbly of himself, and he said, "Indeed, I know of no good in aught that is in me: but because God's word has been said to thee, I can conceal naught from Him to whom nothing is hidden. So then, I shall speak of those things that I am wont to do, set as I am in the midst of many men. It is now thirty years since a bond of continence was agreed between me and my wife and no man knows of it. I have had by her three sons: for them only have I known my wife, nor have I known any other but her, nor herself now at all. I have never ceased to entertain strangers and in such fashion that I let no one go to meet the coming guest before myself. I have never sent a guest from my house without provision for his journey: I have despised no man that was poor, but have supplied him with what things he needed. If I sat in judgment, I have not respected the person of my own son, in detriment of justice. The fruit of another man's toil has never come into my house. If I saw a quarrel, I have never passed by till I brought them that were at odds to peace. No one ever caught my servants in a fault: never have my herds injured another man's crops: never did I forbid any man to sow in my fields, nor did I choose the richer fallow for myself, and leave the more barren to another. As much as in me lay, I never suffered the stronger to oppress the weak. Ever in my life I sought that no one should be sad because of me. If I were judge in a suit, I condemned no one, but sought to bring the dissidents to peace. And this, as God gave it, has been my way of living until now."

And hearing him, the blessed Paphnutius kissed his head and blessed him, saying, "The Lord bless thee out of Zion and mayst thou behold the good things that are in Jerusalem. But as thou hast well and wisely performed all these, one thing thou lackest,

which is the highest of all good, that leaving all thou shouldst
follow the very wisdom of God, and seek the more hidden treasure, whereto thou mayst not come unless thou deny thyself and
take up thy cross, and follow Christ." And when he had heard
this, he delayed for naught, nor sought to set his house in order,
but followed the man of God, taking the road to the desert. . . .
And when some time had gone by, and he had been led to that
perfection of knowledge who was already made perfect in deed,
on a certain day Paphnutius sitting in his cell saw his soul taken
up into heaven amid a host of angels that were saying, *"Blessed is
the man whom Thou choosest and causest to approach unto Thee: he
shall abide in Thy tabernacle."* And hearing this, he knew that the
man had been taken from this world. But Paphnutius persisted
in fasting and prayer, reaching out to things greater and more
perfect.

And again he prayed to God, that he would shew him his fellow among men. And again a divine voice answered him saying:
"Thou art like this merchant, whom thou shalt see coming
towards thee: but rise up quickly and run to meet him, for the
man who is thy fellow is nigh." And going down without delay
Paphnutius met a certain merchant of Alexandria, that was
bringing goods worth twenty thousand pieces of gold in three
ships from the Thebaid. And being a religious man and zealous
after good, he had laden his young men with ten sacks of vegetables, and was bringing them to the monastery of the man of
God: and this was the reason of his coming to Paphnutius. And
straightway as he saw him, "What dost thou," he said, "O soul
most precious, and worthy of God? What toil is this with things
of earth, when thy lot and thy fellowship are in heaven? Leave
these to such as are of earth, and think of earth; but do thou be a
tradesman of the Kingdom of God, to which thou art called, and
follow the Saviour, who will soon hereafter take thee to Him-

self." And he with no least hesitation made his young men give all that remained of his goods to the poor (for he had already himself given much away). And following the holy Paphnutius to the desert, he was set by him in that place from which his predecessors had been taken up to God. And in like fashion, instructed by him in all things, he abode in the exercises of the spirit and in studies of the divine wisdom, and in a little while, he also was translated to the assembly of the just.

And not long after whilst Paphnutius himself was ordering his life in these same exercises of supreme austerity and travail, the angel of God stood by him, saying to him, "Come, thou blessed, and enter those everlasting mansions that are prepared for thee. For behold the Prophets are at hand who shall receive thee into their company. This at first I did not reveal to thee lest perchance thou shouldst be puffed up and thy labour be lost." And after these things for one day he lived his life in the body, and when certain priests came to visit him, he made known to them all that the Lord had revealed to him, saying to them that no one in this world ought to be despised, let him be a thief, or an actor on the stage, or one that tilled the ground, and was bound to a wife, or was a merchant and served a trade: for in every condition of human life there are souls that please God and have their hidden deeds wherein He takes delight: whence is it plain that it is not so much profession or habit that is pleasing to God as the sincerity and affection of the soul and honesty of deed. And when he had spoken thus about each in turn, he gave up his spirit.

xvii. In the country around Arsinoë, we saw a certain Serapion, priest and father of many monasteries: under his care he had more than ten thousand monks, in many and diverse congregations, and all of them earned their bread by the work of their hands, and the great part of what they earned, especially at harvest time, they brought to this Father, for the use of the poor. For it was the custom not only among these, but almost all the Egyptian monks, to hire themselves out at harvest time as harvesters, and each one among them would earn eighty measures of corn, more or less, and offer the greater part of it to the poor, so that not only were the hungry folk of that countryside fed, but ships were sent to Alexandria, laden with corn, to be divided among such as were prisoners in gaols, or as were foreigners and in need. For there was not poverty enough in Egypt to consume the fruit of their compassion and their lavishness.

xxi. So we came to Nitria; the place most famous among all the monasteries of Egypt, about thirty-seven miles distant from Alexandria, and named after the neighbouring town in which nitre is collected, as though in the providence of God it was foreseen that in these parts the sins of men would be washed and utterly effaced, even as stains by nitre are cleansed. In this place there are about fifty (or not many less) habitations, set near together and under one father, in some of which many brethren live together, in some a few, in some a brother lives alone: but though they be divided in their dwelling, yet do they abide bound and inseparable in spirit and faith and loving-kindness.

So then, as we were drawing near the place, as soon as they knew that strange brethren were coming, straightway they poured out like a swarm of bees, each from his cell, and ran to meet us, joyous and eager, the most part carrying pitchers of water and bread, because the Prophet rebuking certain folk had said, *"Ye came not forth to meet the children of Israel with bread and water."* And after they had welcomed us, they brought us first with psalms to the church and washed our feet, and one by one dried them with the linen that girded them, as if to disperse the weariness of the road, and in very act to purge the stains of mortal life in the traditional mystery.

But of their humanity, their courtesy, their loving-kindness, what am I to say, when each man of them would have brought us into his own cell, not only to fulfil the due of hospitality, but still more out of humbleness, wherein they are indeed masters, and from gentleness and its kindred qualities which are learned among them with diverse grace but one and the same doctrine, as if they had come apart from the world for this same end. Nowhere have I seen love so in flower, nowhere so quick compassion, or hospitality so eager. And nowhere have I seen such meditation upon Holy Writ or understanding of it, or such discipline of sacred learning: wellnigh might you judge each one of them a doctor in the wisdom of God.

xxii. Beyond this [Mount Nitria] there is another place in the inner desert, about nine miles distant: and this place, by reason of the multitude of cells dispersed through the desert, they call Cellia, The Cells. To this place those who have had their first initiation and who desire to live a remoter life, stripped of all its trappings, withdraw themselves: for the desert is vast, and the cells are sundered from one another by so wide a space, that none is in sight of his neighbour, nor can any voice be heard.

One by one they abide in their cells, a mighty silence and a great quiet among them: only on the Saturday and the Sunday do they come together to church, and there they see each other face to face as folk restored in heaven. If by chance any one is missing in that gathering, straightway they understand that he has been detained by some unevenness of his body and they all go to visit him, not indeed all of them together but at different times, and each carrying with him whatever he may have by him at home that might seem grateful to the sick. But for no other cause dare any disturb the silence of his neighbour, unless perchance to strengthen by a good word, or as it might be to anoint with the comfort of counsel the athletes set for the struggle. Many of them go three and four miles to church, and the distance dividing one cell from another is no less great: but so great is the love that is in them and by so strong affection are they bound towards one another and towards all brethren that they be an example and a wonder to all. So that if any one by chance should desire to dwell with them, as soon as they perceive it, each man offers his own cell.

We saw a certain venerable father among them, Ammon by name, a man in whom God had brought together the whole plenitude of His grace. When you saw the charity that was in him, you would say that you had nowhere seen the like. But if you considered his humility, you would judge that in this gift he was by far more potent than the rest. And again, if it were his patience, or his gentleness or his benignity, you would judge that in these virtues, one by one he so excelled that you knew not which to put foremost. The gift of wisdom and learning was given him by God in such measure that you would well nigh believe none of all the Fathers had gone so far into the courts of all knowledge: and all that saw him confessed that no one had been so received into the secret chamber of the wisdom of God. . . .

So then we saw this man of God in his cell with a wall about it; a cell is easily built in those parts, ample enough, with rough bricks; he had all that was necessary within, and had himself digged out a well. But there came a certain brother, anxious to be near him for his soul's health, and he went to Ammon to ask if there were a small cell vacant anywhere, in which he might live. Then said he, "I shall make inquiry: but until I find one, do thou stay here in this hermitage; I go out even now to see to it." And leaving him with all he had as well as the hermitage, he found himself a poor cell some distance away and settled himself in it, and gave up his entire hermitage and all that was in it to the unwitting brother. But if it happened they were many that came, anxious to be saved, the old man would bring the brethren together, all eager in helping, and build a hermitage in one day. And when one by one the number of cells was complete, those who were to dwell in them were invited to the church under colour of making a feast, and when they were busied within, each of the brethren would bring from his cell such things as were necessary, and furnish the new cells one by one, so that by this community of charity, no utensil or aught that one needs for victuals was wanting, and yet no one knew whose might be the gift. And so on their return at evening, those for whom the cells were prepared found them furnished with all that was needful, and the habitation so provided that they could see no lack.

xxviii. Certain of the Fathers who were there told us that in those parts had shone the two Macarii like the two lights of heaven: of whom one was an Egyptian by race, and the disciple of the blessed Antony, the other of Alexandria. And even as they accorded in the sound of their name, so did they also in the powers of the soul and the magnificence of their heavenly graces. Each of the two was Macarius, each equally valiant in abstinence and powers of the soul, the one excelling the other in this only that he owned as it were by inheritance the grace and goodness of the blessed Antony.

And then they told of him, that at one time in the neighbouring countryside a murder had been committed, and the crime fastened upon an innocent man, and he who was thus under calumny fled for refuge to his cell: and thither came also his persecutors, accusing him and declaring that they themselves were in peril unless they seized the murderer and delivered him over to the law. But he on whom the crime was fastened swore on the sacraments that he was innocent of this man's blood. And while the contention went on, on this side and on that, the holy Macarius asked where he was buried that was reportedly slain. And when they had shown him the place, he set out with all the company that had come to harry the man to the sepulchre; and there upon his knees he invoked the name of Christ, and said to those who stood by: "Now shall the Lord show if the guilty man is indeed this whom ye have accused." And lifting up his voice he called the dead man by name. And when he that was summoned answered from the sepulchre, he said to him, "I charge thee by the faith of Christ, tell us now if it was by this man who bears the blame, that thou wast slain." Then the voice from the grave did clearly answer, that it was not by him he had been slain. And in amazement they all fell to the ground, and they rolled at his feet and began begging him to ask the dead who it was by whom he had been slain. Then said he: "I shall not ask this thing: it is enough for me that the innocent goes free: it is not for me to betray the guilty."

xxix. They said that he [Macarius of Alexandria] was a lover beyond all other men of the desert, and had explored its ultimate and inaccessible wastes. . . . The place in which the holy Macarius lived was called Scete. It is set in a vast desert, a day and a night's journey from the monasteries on Nitria, and the way to it is to be found or shown by no track and no landmarks of earth, but one journeys by the signs and courses of the stars. Water is hard to find, and when it is found it is of a dire odour and as it might be bituminous, yet inoffensive in taste. Here therefore are men made perfect in holiness (for so terrible a spot could be endured by none save those of austere resolve and supreme constancy), yet their chief concern is the love which they show to one another and toward such as by chance reach that spot.

They tell that once a certain brother brought a bunch of grapes to the holy Macarius: but he who for love's sake thought not on his own things but on the things of others, carried it to another brother, who seemed more feeble. And the sick man gave thanks to God for the kindness of his brother, but he too thinking more of his neighbour than of himself, brought it to another, and he again to another, and so that same bunch of grapes was carried round all the cells, scattered as they were far over the desert, and no one knowing who first had sent it, it was brought at last to the first giver. But the holy Macarius gave thanks that he had seen in the brethren such abstinence and such loving-kindness and did himself reach after still sterner discipline of the life of the spirit.

THE SAYINGS OF
THE FATHERS

translated from the Greek by Pelagius the Deacon
and John the Subdeacon

The *Verba Seniorum,* the Sayings of the Fathers, are the kernel of the desert tradition. To come to them through Jerome, Rufinus, Palladius, Cassian, is like coming to the Gospels through the Epistles, to the oral as distinct from the literary tradition. For though Jerome and his company knew the desert at first hand, they put style on it: they are men of letters, cursed with a feeling for prose. Moreover, it is the desert through the medium of a temperament: Jerome cannot do without his period, Cassian his devout reflection, Rufinus his warm sentiment, Palladius his gossip. But the compiler of the Greek original which Pelagius translated does not suffer even his shadow to fall across the page. Not even in the brief chapter-headings is the reader conscious of a later disposing hand. There is no attempt at characterisation; if he once uses the word "great," it is in the reported speech of another. "The abbot Antony said. . . . The abbot Arsenius said. . . . Certain of the old men used to tell. . . ." It is as near as the written word can come to the nakedness of the living voice.

In this again like the Gospels, the identity of the *Verba Seniorum* all but disappeared behind the sandstorm of controversy that broke loose in the last decades of the nineteenth century. On the question of priority of text—Greek, Latin, Syriac, Coptic, Aramaic, Arabic—it rages still, but in the heart of the whirlwind there is quiet. There, in the abbé Brémond's enchanting vision, sit the great antagonists, in the cell of Paphnutius or Poemen, fervent and docile, each on his little stool of reeds.[1] However multifarious the versions, the source is one, the desert of Scete, to which one journeyed only by the signs and courses of the stars: and the voices are for the most part the voices of men who lived there between the middle of the fourth and the middle of the fifth century. In Scete, as in Galilee, says Père Lebreton, "the phrases are struck out with such vigour that they engrave themselves upon the heart; they are repeated, and the oral tradition little by little takes shape in the written collections [there was one already in existence, made by Evagrius, before 400]; and in both cases one finds a similar transposition from the vulgar tongue, Aramaic or Coptic, into the literary language, the Greek."[2] Jerome in the Syrian desert clamoured for letters from his friends, "for they talk with me, they at least know Latin; here one must learn this barbarious half-language, or hold one's tongue."[3] Yet it is not to be assumed that the Fathers whose speech is recorded were all of them either Egyptian or illiterate. Arsenius was reckoned a scholar both in Constantinople and in Rome, a master of both Greek and Latin,[4] like the silent Theon of the Thebaid, who walked in the desert at night with the wild things of the desert walking by his side:[5] Marcus was an elegant scribe,[6] Evagrius Ponticus the author of several books (one, *On Invulnerability,* which Rufinus translated, was dismissed by Jerome with the gibe that whoever attained to that pitch of insensibility was either a stone or God).[7] Yet Arsenius' friend was a shepherd that had never lived in any town, and when another wondered at it, he made answer that he had indeed laid hold on the learning of Greece and Rome, as this world goes, but knew not even the alphabet of his shepherd's wisdom.[8]

There is one famous collection in Greek, in which the sayings of each Father are grouped under his name, and the whole alphabetically arranged, so that it becomes a dictionary of little biographies.[9] Yet the result is rather that of a necrology, a *hortus siccus* in place of Jerome's "desert of flowers in spring, desert that art God's familiar."[10] The text that Pelagius translated in the sixth century, and that all mediæval Europe knew, and copied and recopied, was grouped under subjects—"That a man should possess naught"; "that a man should in no wise judge his neighbour"—and the word passes from Arsenius, the arbitrary haunted aristocrat, to Moses, the "long black man" who was converted from among the robbers, and was liable to gibes about his colour, and Zachary, eloquently silent, and Theodore, whose speech was like a sword, and Nistero that had known Antony, or "a certain old man," as anonymous as the compiler.

His complete self-abnegation had its power over his translators, Pelagius the Deacon, and John the Subdeacon. It is generally accepted that the first is that Pelagius who became Pope in 555, an excellent Greek scholar and one that had been much employed in ecclesiastical embassies to the Eastern Church. He stopped midway in the eighteenth chapter, possibly because his accession to St. Peter's chair with its administrative burden left him no time to "tread again the ancient track." But John the Subdeacon took up the work, and finally succeeded him in the Papacy as well as in the translation.[11] They wrote in perhaps the worst period of inflation, alike of sentiment and of language: but especially with Pelagius, the austerity of the original possessed him, and the Latin has an archaic simplicity. The same thing is to be observed of Jerome, in the presence of Holy

Writ. His taste, as in the *Life of St. Paul the Hermit,* could some-times be execrable: but in the Vulgate he sacrifices his style, and even the grammar that Donatus taught him in Rome,[12] to give as exact a tracing as he can of the very structure of the original, as well as of its meaning, so that one will find him writing *Dixit ad eos* instead of *Dixit iis,* the better to level at the Greek.

For the place, Mount Nitria is above the Wâdî an-Natrûn, south of Lake Mareotis, which lies between it and Alexandria; it took Palladius a day and a half to cross the lake. Nitria, he said, was at the edge of deserts that stretched as far Ethiopia, and Mauretania, and the country of the Mazaci. Cellia was nine miles deeper in the desert, Scete forty miles, with no track lead-ing to it.[13] The domestic conditions can be pieced together from the stories: a hut of stones with a roof of branches from the marsh, but with a door at which visitors knocked, and which could be locked;[14] a reed mat for a bed, a reed stool for a seat by day and a pillow at night;[15] a sheepskin. If one moved house, one took one's sheepskin; it seemed enough. There was a fire, for Pa-chomius when he lived as disciple with old Palæmon would go out to gather wood, and when the thorns pierced his feet, he called to mind Christ's Passion: and a boastful visitor arrived one night, as he and the old man were kindling the fire for their nightly vigil.[16] There was a lamp, or sometimes a candlestick, and a jar of oil for the lamp, and one, that might be a present, of honey; dry peas and lentils that could be steeped; a jar of wine for a visitor, brackish water for one's self. A jar with water to steep the palm leaves for the baskets and mats which one sold one's self in the market, or got the sacristan to sell. If the water were not changed, it stank, probably like flaxwater along the Irish roads: the brethren complained of the smell of it in Arse-nius' hut. In the window, if the occupant were a scholar, a codex;

the window-ledge is the bookshelf of cottar houses in Ireland to this day. Round the house might be a herb garden: the harsher anchorites deprecated it, but Antony himself planted one, and begged the wild asses not to damage it.[17] The bread hung in a basket, or might be stored in a cupboard.[18] Poor as the furnishing was, desert thieves came to pillage. Macarius came home to find one in his hut, and stood by like an obliging stranger, and helped the thief to load his animal and finally led him out, making no noise; but Macarius, the brethren said, was like God, who shields the world and bears its sin; so did he shield the brethren, and when a man sinned, he would neither hear nor see.

One note on a point of translation: the word *abbas* used by Pelagius for the senior and more reverend dwellers in the desert is a difficult one. The nearest approach to its meaning here is probably the Hebrew Rabbi, or the affectionate respect of the French *Maitre*. "Father" in this connotation is too modern; yet "abbot" means the head of a religious community, and many of these were solitaries. That in spite of this I have kept to the literal translation is partly because Pelagius himself chose it in preference to *pater*, and partly because it echoes the *abba* of the Gospels.

BOOK I
Of the Perfecting of the Fathers

i. A certain man asked the abbot Antony, saying, "What shall I keep, that I may please God?" And the old man answering said, "These things that I bid thee, do thou keep. Wherever thou goest, have God ever before thine eyes: in what thou dost, hold by the example of the holy Scriptures: and in whatever place thou dost abide, be not swift to remove from thence. These three things keep, and thou shalt be saved."

ii. The abbot Pambo asked the abbot Antony, saying, "What shall I do?" And the old man made answer, "Be not confident of thine own righteousness: grieve not over a thing that is past: and be continent of thy tongue and of thy belly."

iv. The abbot Evagrius said, "Certain of the Fathers used to say that a dry and even diet joined together with loving-kindness shall speedily bring the monk into the harbour of invulnerability."

xi. A brother asked an old man, saying, "What thing is there so good that I may do it and live?" And the old man said, "God alone knoweth what is good: yet I have heard that one of the Fathers questioned the great abbot Nistero, who was friend to abbot Antony, and said, 'What good work shall I do?' And he answered, 'All works are not equal. The Scripture saith that Abraham was hospitable, and God was with him. And Elias loved quiet, and God was with him. And David was humble, and God was with him. What therefore thou findest that thy soul desireth in following God, that do, and keep thy heart.'"

xv. The abbot Pastor said, "If a monk will hate two things, he can be free from this world." And a brother said, "What are they?" And the old man, "Relaxation of the body, and vainglory."

xvi. They said of the abbot Pambo, that in that hour of his departing from this life, he said to the holy men that stood about him, "From the time that I came into this place of solitude and built my cell, and dwelt in it, I do not call to mind that I have eaten bread save what my hands have toiled for, nor repented of any word that I spoke until this hour. And so I go to the Lord, as one that hath not yet made a beginning of serving God."

xix. A brother asked an old man, "How cometh the fear of God in a man?" And the old man said, "If a man have humility and poverty and judgeth not another, so comes in him the fear of God."

BOOK II
Of Quiet

i. The abbot Antony said, "Fish, if they tarry on dry land, die: even so monks that tarry outside their cell or abide with men of the world fall away from their vow of quiet. As a fish must return to the sea, so must we to our cell: lest it befall that by tarrying without, we forget the watch within."

ii. The abbot Antony said, "Who sits in solitude and is quiet hath escaped from three wars: hearing, speaking, seeing: yet against one thing shall he continually battle: that is, his own heart."

iii. The abbot Arsenius when he was still in the palace, prayed to God, saying, "Lord, show me the way of deliverance." And a voice came to him saying, "Arsenius, flee from men, and thou shalt be saved." And departing to the monastic life, he prayed again, saying the same words. And he heard a voice saying to him, "Arsenius, flee, hold thy peace, be still: for these are the roots of sinning not."

iv. The archbishop Theophilus of blessed memory came once to the abbot Arsenius, with a certain judge. And the archbishop questioned the old man, desiring to hear some word from him. For a while the old man was silent, and thereafter replied to him, saying, "And if I tell you aught, will ye keep it?" They promised that they would keep it. And the old man said to them, "Wheresoever ye shall hear of Arsenius, come not nigh."

Another time the archbishop desiring to see him, sent first to know if he would open the door to him. And he sent him word saying, "If thou comest, I shall open to thee. But if I have opened the door to thee, I open to all, and then I shall dwell no longer in this place." And hearing it, the archbishop said, "If I go to persecute him, I shall go to the holy man no more."

v. At one time the abbot Arsenius came to a certain place and there was a bed of reeds, and the reeds were shaken by the wind. And the old man said to the brethren, "What is this rustling?" And they said, "It is the reeds." The old man said to them, "Verily, if a man sits in quiet and hears the voice of a bird, he hath not the same quiet in his heart: how much more shall it be with you, that hear the sound of these reeds?"

vi. They also said of him that his cell was thirty miles away, and that he did not leave it readily, but others did his errands. But when the place which is called Scete was laid waste, he went away weeping and saying, "The world destroyed Rome, and the monks Scete."

vii. At one time when the abbot Arsenius was living in Canopus, there came from Rome in hope to see him a lady, a virgin, of great wealth, and one that feared God: and Theophilus the archbishop received her. And she prayed him to use his good offices with the old man, that she might see him. And the archbishop came to him and asked him, saying, "A certain lady hath come from Rome, and would see thee." But the old man would not consent to have her come to him. So when this was told the lady, she commanded her beasts to be saddled, saying, "I trust in God, that I shall see him. For in my own city there are men to spare: but I am come to see the prophets." And when she came to the old man's cell, by the ordering of God it chanced that he was found outside his cell. And when the lady saw him, she cast herself at his feet. But with indignation did he raise her up; and gazing upon her, said, "If thou dost desire to look upon my face, here am I: look." But she for shame did not lift her eyes to his face. And the old man said to her, "Hast thou not heard what I do? To see the work is enough. How didst thou dare to take upon thee so great a voyage? Dost thou not know that thou art a woman, and ought not to go anywhere? And wilt thou now go to Rome and say to the other women, 'I have seen Arsenius,' and turn the sea into a high road of women coming to me?" But she said, "If God will that I return to Rome, I shall let no woman come hither. But pray for me, and always remember me." He answered and said, "I pray God that He will wipe the memory of thee from my heart." And hearing this, she went away troubled. And when she had come back into the city, she fell into a fever for sorrow. And it was told the archbishop that she was sick: and he came to comfort her, and asked her what ailed her. And she said to him, "Would that I had not come hither! For I said to the old man, 'Remember me.' And he said to me, 'I pray God that He will wipe the memory of thee from my heart,' and behold I am dying of that sorrow." And the archbishop said to her, "Knowest thou not that thou art a woman, and through women doth the Enemy lay siege to holy men? For this reason did the old man say it, but he doth ever pray for thy soul." And so her mind was healed. And she departed with joy to her own place.

ix. A certain brother came to the abbot Moses in Scete seeking a word from him. And the old man said to him, "Go and sit in thy cell, and thy cell shall teach thee all things."

xi. The abbot Nilus said, "Invulnerable from the arrows of the enemy is he who loves quiet: but he who mixeth with the crowd hath often wounds."

xiv. The abbess Matrona said, ... "It is better to have many about thee, and to live the solitary life in thy will, than to be alone, and the desire of thy mind be with the crowd."

xvi. A certain one told this story: There were three earnest men, that loved one another, and they became monks. And one of them chose to bring to accord such as take the law of each other, according to that which is written: *Blessed are the peacemakers.* The second chose to visit the sick. But the third went away to be quiet in solitude. Now the first toiling amid the contentions of men was not able to appease them all. And overcome with weariness he came to him who tended the sick, and found him also failing in spirit, and unable to carry out his purpose. And the two agreed together and went away to see him who had withdrawn into the desert, and they told him their tribulations. And they asked him to tell them how he himself had fared. And he was silent for awhile, and then poured water into a vessel and said, "Look upon the water." And it was murky. And after a little while he said again, "Look now, how clear the water has become." And as they looked into the water they saw their own faces, as in a mirror. And then he said to them, "So is he who abides in the midst of men: because of the turbulence, he sees not his sins: but when he hath been quiet, above all in solitude, then does he recognize his own default."

BOOK III
Of Compunction

iv. The abbot Elias said, "Three things I fear: the first, what time my soul shall go forth from my body; the second, what time I shall go to meet God; the third, what time the sentence shall go forth against me."

v. The archbishop Theophilus of holy memory when he was dying said, "Blessed art thou, abbot Arsenius, who hadst ever this hour before thine eyes."

x. At one time the abbot Pastor was in Egypt, and passing by he saw a woman sitting on a grave and bitterly weeping, and he said, "If all the delights of this world should come by, they could not carry the soul of that woman from grief. So should the monk for ever have grief in his heart."

xiii. A brother asked him, saying, "What shall I do?" And he said, "When Abraham came into the land of promise, he prepared for himself a sepulchre, and secured for an inheritance ground enough for a grave." And the brother said, "What means a sepulchre?" And the old man said, "A place of weeping and sorrow."

xiv. Athanasius of holy memory besought the abbot Pambo to come down from the desert to Alexandria; and when he had come down, he saw there a woman that was an actress, and he wept. And when those who stood by asked him wherefore he had wept he spoke. "Two things," said he, "moved me. One, her perdition; the other, that I have not so much concern to please God as she hath to please vile men."

xvi. Syncletica of holy memory said, "Sore is the toil and struggle of the unrighteous when they turn to God, and afterwards is joy ineffable. For even as with those who would kindle a fire, they first are beset with smoke, and from the pain of the smoke they weep, and so they come at what they desired. Even so is it written, *'Our God is a consuming fire'*: and needs must we kindle the divine fire in us with travail and with tears."

xxiii. An old man saw one laughing, and said to him, "In presence of Heaven and earth we are to give account of our whole life to God; and thou dost laugh?"

xxv. A brother asked an old man saying, "Father, give me

some word." The old man said to him, "When God struck Egypt, there was no house that had not mourning."

BOOK IV
Of Self-Restraint

i. Certain brethren, being minded to go from Scete to the abbot Antony, went aboard a ship that they might go to him: and they found in that same ship an old man who likewise was minded to go to Antony. But the brethren did not know him. And as they sat in the ship they talked with one another about the sayings of the Fathers and about the Scriptures, and again about the work that they did with their hands. But the old man held his peace through all. When they reached the harbour, they perceived that the old man also was on his way to the abbot Antony. And when they had come to him, the abbot Antony said to them, "Ye found a good companion for your journey in this old man." And he also said to the old man, "Thou didst find good brethren to company thee, Father." Then said the old man, "Indeed they be good, but their house hath no door. Whosoever will, may enter into the stable and loose the ass." Now he said this because whatsoever came into their hearts, that they spoke with their mouths.

ii. The abbot Daniel said of the abbot Arsenius, that he would spend the night in vigil. All the night through he waked, and when toward morning he craved for very nature to sleep, he would say to sleep, "Come, thou ill servant," and would snatch a little sleep, sitting: and straightway would rise up.

iii. The abbot Arsenius said, "It sufficeth a monk if he sleep for one hour: that is, if he be a fighter."

iv. The abbot Daniel said of him, "For so many years did he

live with us, and we gave him a scant portion of food in the year: and every time we would come to visit him, it was ourselves that ate it."

v. He said again that not more than once a year did he change the water for steeping the palm-leaves, but only added to it. And he would make a plait of those palm-leaves and stitch it until the sixth hour. The fathers asked him once why he did not change the palm-water, because it stank. And he said to them, "For the incense and the fragrance of the perfumes that I used in the world, needs must I use this stench now."

viii. At one time the abbot Agatho was on a journey with his disciples. And one of them found a little bundle of green peas on the road and said to the old man, "Father, if thou wilt, I shall lift that." The old man looked at him wonderingly, and said, "Didst thou put it there?" The brother answered, "No." And the old man said, "How couldst thou wish to lift up that which thou didst not put down?"

x. At one time the abbot Achilles came into the cell of the abbot Isaiah, in Scete, and found him eating. For he had put salt and water in the pot. And seeing that he hid it behind plaits of palm-leaves he said to him, "Tell me what thou was eating." He answered, "Forgive me, Father, but I was cutting palm-leaves and I grew hot: and so I dipped a morsel of bread in salt and put it into my mouth: and my throat was parched and the morsel did not go down that I had put into my mouth, and so I was compelled to pour a little water upon the salt, so that I could swallow it: but forgive me." And the abbot Achilles used to say, "Come and see Isaiah supping broth in Scete. If thou wouldst sup broth, go down into Egypt."

xii. The abbot Benjamin, who was a priest in Cellae, said that he once came to a certain old man in Scete and would have given him a little oil, but he said to him, "Look where sitteth the little jar that thou didst bring me three years ago: and just as thou didst set it down, so it hath remained." And he heard it and marvelled at the manner of life of the old man.

xv. At one time Epiphanius bishop of Cyprus sent to the abbot Hilarion, asking him and saying, "Come that I may see thee, before I go forth from the body." And when they had come together, and were eating, a portion of fowl was brought them: and the bishop took it and gave to the abbot Hilarion. And the old man said to him, "Forgive me, Father, but from the time that I took this habit, I have eaten naught that hath been killed." And Epiphanius said to him, "And I from the time that I took this habit have let no man sleep that had aught against me, nor have I slept holding aught against any man." And the old man said to him, "Forgive me, for thy way of life is greater than mine."

xx. The abbot John of short stature said, "Once when I was climbing up the road that leads to Scete with palm-leaf mats, I saw a camel-driver, and he began speaking and rousing me to fury. And I dropped what I was carrying and fled."

xxi. Said the abbot Isaac, priest at Cellae, "I know a brother that was harvesting in the field, and was fain to eat an ear of wheat. And he said to the owner of the field, 'Wilt thou suffer me to eat one ear?' And hearing him he marvelled and said to him, 'Father, the field is thine, and dost thou ask me?' So scrupulous was this brother."

xxii. One of the brethren asked the abbot Isidore, an old man in Scete, saying, "Wherefore do the devils fear thee so mightily?" And the old man said to him, "From the time that I was made a monk, I have striven not to suffer anger to mount as far as my throat."

xxvi. They told of the abbot Macarius that if he were making holiday with the brethren, and wine was brought, and he drank for the brethren's sake, he set this bond upon himself that for one cup of wine, he would drink no water for a whole day. And the brethren, eager to give him pleasure, would bring him wine. And the old man would take it joyously, to torment himself thereafter. But his disciple, knowing the reason, said to the brethren, "For God's sake do not give it him, for he brings under his body with torments thereafter in his cell." And the brethren when they know it gave him wine no more.

xxvii. The abbot Macarius the elder used to say to the brethren in Scete, "When mass is ended in the church, flee, my brothers." And one of the brethren said to him, "Father, whither in this solitude can we further flee?" And he laid his finger upon his mouth saying, "This is what I would have you flee." And so he would go into his cell and shut the door and there sit alone.

xxviii. And again the abbot Macarius said, "If in desiring to rebuke any one thou art thyself moved to anger, thou dost satisfy thine own passion; in saving another, lose not thyself."

xlix. The abbot Hyperichius said, "The monk that cannot master his tongue in time of anger will not be master of the passions of his body at some other time."

li. He said again, "It is better to eat flesh and to drink wine than to eat the flesh of the brethren by backbiting them."

liv. Another time a vessel of wine, the first of the vintage, was brought in, and cups apiece were given to the brethren. And a certain brother coming in, and seeing that they were taking wine, fled into the crypt, and the crypt fell in. And when they heard the noise, they ran and found the brother lying half dead and began to revile him, saying, "Rightly did this befall thee, for thy vainglorying." But the abbot, cherishing him, said, "Leave my son alone, he did a good deed. And as the Lord liveth, that crypt shall not be built again in my time, that the world may know that for a cup of wine a crypt fell in Scete."

lv. At one time a priest from Scete went up to visit the bishop of Alexandria. And when he came back to Scete, the brethren questioned him, "How fares the city?" But he answered them, "Believe me, my brothers, I saw no man's face there, not even the face of the bishop." And on hearing this they marvelled and said, "What thinkest thou hath become of all that multitude?" And the priest resolved their doubts, saying, "I wrested away my soul, that I might not look upon the face of man." And the brothers profited by the story, and guarded themselves against lifting up their eyes.

lvi. There once came a certain old man to another old man. And he said to his disciple, "Cook us some lentils." And he did so. "And steep some bread for us." And he steeped it. And they so remained till the sixth hour of the day following, speaking of the things of the spirit. And again the old man said to his disciple, "Cook us some lentils, my son." He answered, "It has been done since yesterday." And so they rose and ate their food.

lxi. At one time a brother went to visit his sister that lay ill in the convent. Now she was of great devotion. And being unwilling ever to see man, or to bring her brother into temptation by his coming for her sake into the midst of women, she sent him word, saying, "Go, my brother, and pray for me: for by Christ's grace I shall see thee in the kingdom of Heaven."

lxii. A monk met the handmaids of God upon a certain road, and at the sight of them he turned out of the way. And the Abbess said to him, "Hadst thou been a perfect monk thou wouldst not have looked so close as to perceive that we were women."

lxiv. A certain brother brought fresh loaves into his cell, and invited his elders to table. And when they had eaten a farl apiece, they stopped. But the brother, knowing their travail of abstinence, began humbly to entreat them, saying, "For God's sake, eat this day until ye be filled." And they ate another ten. Behold therefore how these that were true monks and sincere in abstinence did eat more than they had need of, for God's sake.

lxvi. An old man had lived long in the desert, and it chanced that a brother came to see him, and found him ill. And he washed his face and made him a meal of the things he had brought with him. And when the old man saw it, he said, "Indeed, brother, I had forgotten what solace men may have in food." He offered him also a cup of wine. And when he saw it, he wept, saying, "I had not thought to drink wine until I died."

lxviii. A certain brother was going on a journey, and he had his mother with him, and she was old. They came to a certain river, and the old woman could not cross it. And her son took off his cloak and wrapped it about his hands, lest he should in any wise touch the body of his mother, and so carrying her, he set her on the other side of the stream. Then said his mother to him, "Why didst thou so cover thy hands, my son?" He answered, "Because the body of a woman is fire. And even from my touching thee, came the memory of other women into my soul."

BOOK V
Of Fornication

iv. There was a certain brother that was earnest and anxious after good living. And being sorely harassed by the demon of lust, he came to a certain old man and related to him his imaginings.

But on hearing them, and himself being free, the old man was wroth, and declared that the brother was vile and unworthy to wear the habit of a monk, inasmuch as he admitted such thoughts to his mind. And the brother, hearing this, despaired of himself: and he left his own cell and took the road back to the world. But by God's providence the abbot Apollo met him: and seeing him perturbed and in heavy sadness, questioned him, saying, "My son, what is the cause of this deep sadness of thine?" At first the brother, in the shame of his soul, could answer him nothing: but after the old man had asked him many questions as to what had befallen him, he confessed, saying, "Thoughts of lust do harry me: and I confessed it to this old man, and according to him there is now no hope of salvation for me: and so in despair of myself I am going back to the world."

But when the abbot Apollo heard this, like a wise physician he began asking many questions and counselled him, saying, "Think it no strange thing, my son, nor despair of thyself. For I myself, at my age, and in this way of life, am sorely harried by just such thoughts as these. Wherefore be not found wanting in this kind of testing, where the remedy is not so much in man's anxious thought as in God's compassion. Today at least grant me what I ask of thee, and go back to thy cell." And the brother did so. But the abbot Apollo on leaving him made his way to the cell of that old man who had brought him to despair: and standing without he entreated God with tears, saying, "Lord, who dost send temptation when it is needed, turn the battle wherein that brother has suffered against this old man that by experience he may learn in his old age what length of time has never taught him: to have compassion on those who are harassed by temptations of this sort." His prayer ended, he saw an Ethiopian standing close to the cell and shooting arrows against the old man: and as if pierced by them, the old man was borne hither and thither like a man drunk with wine. And when he could endure it no longer, he came out of his cell and down that same road which the young man had taken, going back to the world.

But the abbot Apollo, understanding what had befallen, went to meet him. And coming up to him, he said, "Whither goest thou? And what is the cause of the trouble which hath seized thee?" But he, feeling that the holy man knew what had befallen him, could not speak for shame. Then said the abbot Apollo, "Go back to thy cell and for the rest, recognise thy weakness and look to thyself: for either the devil hath forgotten thee until now, or was contemptuous of thee, inasmuch as thou hast never been found worthy, like men of valour, to do battle with the enemy. Battle, did I say?—thou who couldst not stand against his onset for a single day. But this hath befallen thee, because when that young man, beset by our common adversary, came to thee, instead of anointing him with words of comfort against the struggle, thou didst send him to desperation, with not a thought of that most wise counsel that bids us deliver those who are drawn down to death, and neglect not to redeem the falling: nor yet the parable of Our Saviour when He said, *The bruised reed thou shalt not break, the smoking flax thou shalt not quench.* For no man can endure the assaults of the adversary, neither can any extinguish or restrain the fire that leaps in our nature, unless God's grace shall give its strength to human weakness. In this salutary judgment upon us, let us pray to God with all supplication, that He will turn aside the scourge that is fallen upon thee, for He maketh sore and bindeth up: He woundeth and His hands make whole: He bringeth low and lifteth up: He killeth and maketh alive: He bringeth down to hell and bringeth back." And so saying, he made his prayer, and straightway was the old man freed from the warfare that had been brought upon him. And the abbot Apollo counselled him to ask of God for the tongue of the wise that he might know when it was time to speak.

v. The abbot Cyrus of Alexandria, questioned as to the imagination of lust, made answer: "If thou hast not these imaginings, thou art without hope: for if thou hast not the imagination thereof, thou hast the deed itself. For he who fights not in his mind against sin, nor gainsays it, sins in the flesh. And he who sins in the flesh, hath no trouble from the imagination thereof."

vi. An old man questioned a brother, saying, "Is it not thy wont to have speech with women?" And the brother said, "Nay. But my imagination and certain memories I have are painters old and new, disquieting me with images of women." And the old man said to him, "Fear not the dead, but flee the living: that is to say, the consenting to, and the act of, sin: and give thyself longer to prayer."

ix. At one time a brother came to the abbot Pastor, and said to him, "What am I to do, Father? For I am harried with lust. And I sought out the abbot Hybistion, and he said to me, 'Thou oughtst not to allow it to tarry long in thee.'" And the abbot Pastor said to him, "The deeds of the abbot Hybistion are above with the angels in heaven: but thou and I are in fleshly lust. But if a monk keep his belly and his tongue and stay in solitude, he may have confidence that he will not die."

xiii. Another brother was goaded by lust, and rising at night he made his way to an old man, and told him his thoughts, and the old man comforted him. And revived by that comforting he returned to his cell. And again the spirit of lust tempted him, and again he went to the old man. And this happened many times. But the old man did not discountenance him, but spoke to him to his profit, saying, "Yield not to the devil, nor relax thy mind: but rather as often as the devil troubles thee, come to me, and he shall go buffeted away. For nothing so dispirits the demon of lust as when his assaults are revealed. And nothing so heartens him as when his imaginations are kept secret." So the brother came to him eleven times, confessing his imaginings. And thereafter he said to the old man, "Show love to me, my father, and give me some word." The old man said, "Believe me, my son, if God permitted the thoughts with which my own mind is stung to be transferred to thee, thou wouldst not endure them, but wouldst dash thyself headlong." And by the old man saying this, his great humbleness did quiet the goading of lust in the brother.

xix. A certain brother, bound by the spirit of lust, made his way to a certain great old man and asked him, saying, "Show me kindness and pray for me, for I am harried by lust." So the old man entreated the Lord for him. And again coming to the old man, he told the same tale. And again the old man did not neglect to beseech the Lord for him, saying, "Lord, reveal to me whence cometh this devil's work in my brother. For I have prayed Thee for him, and he hath not yet found any peace." And the Lord revealed to him what was happening round about that brother. The old man saw him sitting and the spirit of lust beside him as it were sporting with him, and an Angel sent to his help was standing by, and indignant against that brother because he did not prostrate himself before God, but was as one delighting in his imaginations and his whole mind inclining to them. And the old man perceived that the fault was with the brother, and told him so, saying, "Thou dost consent to thine imagination." And he taught him how one must withstand such thoughts. And the brother, taking breath again by the old man's wisdom and prayer, found peace from his temptation.

xxvii. Two brethren made their way to the city to sell their handiwork: and when in the city they went different ways, divided one from the other, one of them fell into fornication. After a while came his brother, saying, "Brother, let us go back to our cell." But he made answer, "I am not coming." And the other questioned him, saying, "Wherefore, brother?" And he answered, "Because when thou didst go from me, I ran into temptation, and I sinned in the flesh." But the other, anxious to help him, began to tell him, saying, "But so it happened with me: when I was separated from thee, I too ran into fornication. But let us go, and do penance together with all our might: and God will forgive us that are sinful men." And they came back to the monastery and told the old men what had befallen them, and they enjoined on them the penance they must do. But the one began his penance, not for himself but for his brother, as if he himself had sinned. And God, seeing his love and his labour, after a few days revealed to one of the old men that for the great love of this brother who had not sinned, He had forgiven the brother who had. And verily this is to lay down one's soul for one's brother.

xxviii. A brother once came to a certain old man, saying, "My brother is destroying me for ever going hither and thither; and I am in distress over him." And the old man questioned him, saying, "Take it with a quiet mind, my brother, and God, seeing thy work of patience, will call him back to thee. For it is not possible that by dint of harshness and austerity a man shall lightly be recalled from his intent: for devils do not cast out devils: but by gentleness shalt thou call him back to thee. For by such means as this doth our God draw men to Himself." And he told him a story: how there were two brethren in the Thebaid, and one of them would have run into fornication, and said to his fellow, "I am going back to the world." But the other wept and said, "I will not let thee go, brother, and lose thy labour and thy virginity." But he would not agree, and said, "I will not sit here: I am going. Either come with me and I shall come back with thee again, or else let me go, and I shall stay in the world." So the brother went and told a certain old man. And the old man said, "Go with him, and God for thy travail will not let him go to ruin." So he rose up and went away with his brother to the world. And when he had reached a certain town, God, seeing his travail, how from love and necessity he was following his brother, removed desire from his brother's heart. And he said, "Brother, let us go back to the desert. Behold, I think to myself, 'Now I have sinned with a woman': what better am I of that?" And turning about, they came back unharmed to their cell.

xxix. A brother tempted by a demon set out to a certain old man and said to him, "These two brothers are together, and they are of evil life." But the old man perceived that he was beguiled of the devil, and he sent and called them to him. And when evening was come, he laid down a mat for the two brethren, and happed them in one bed, saying, "The sons of God are great and holy." But he said to his disciple, "Shut that brother into a cell by himself: for the passion which he would fasten on them he hath in himself."

xxxi. A certain brother questioned an old man about imaginings of this kind. And the old man said to him, "I myself have never been goaded by this thing." And the brother was scandalized at him and went off to another old man saying, "Behold, this is what the old man said to me, and I was scandalized at him: for what he says is beyond nature." And the old man said, "Not in foolishness was this said to thee by the man of God: arise and go, and do penance before him, that he may open to thee the wisdom in his words." So the brother rose up and came to the old man, and did penance in his sight. And he said, "Forgive me, Father, in that I behaved like a fool, and left thee without bidding thee farewell: but I entreat thee to explain to me how thou hast never been harried by lust." The old man said to him, "Since the time that I became a monk I have never given myself my fill of bread, nor of water, nor of sleep, and tormenting myself with appetite for these things whereby we are fed, I was not suffered to feel the stings of lust." And the brother went away, profiting by the old man's tale.

xxxvii. There was a certain solitary living in Lower Egypt, and his fame was known to all, because alone in the church he dwelt in a desert place. And behold, by the operation of Satan a certain woman of ill fame heard of him and said to the young men, "What will ye give me if I bring down this solitary of yours?" And they agreed with her what they would surely give her. She went out at evening, and came as one that had lost her way, to his cell: and when she knocked at his door, he came out. And seeing her he was troubled, saying, "How hast thou come here?" And she answered him as if weeping and said, "I lost my way and so came here." And he was shaken with pity for her, and brought her into the courtyard about his cell and himself went into his cell and shut the door. And the unhappy creature cried out, saying, "Father, the wild beasts are devouring me." Again he was troubled, fearing the judgments of God, and said, "Whence cometh this wrath upon me?" And opening the door, he brought her within.

Then began the devil to pierce his heart as with arrows to desire her. And when he felt that these desires were of the devil, he said within himself, "The ways of the enemy are darkness: but the Son of God is light."

Rising, he lit the lamp. And when he burnt with desire, he

said, "They that do these things go into torment. Prove thyself now, from this, if thou canst bear the everlasting fire." And he put his finger into the flame, and when it burnt and scorched he felt it not, for the flame of lust that was in him. And so when daylight broke, all his fingers were burned. But when the unhappy woman saw what he was doing, she became like a stone for dread.

In the morning, the young men came to the monk, and asked him, "Did a woman come here last evening?" He said, "Yea: see, there she sleeps." And coming in they found her dead. And they said, "Father, she is dead."

Then, turning back the cloak that he wore, he showed them his hands, saying, "See what yon daughter of the devil hath done to me, she hath cost me every finger I have." And telling them what had come to pass, he said, "It is written, 'Render not evil for evil.'" And he prayed, and raised her up. And she turned from her sins and lived in chastity for the rest of her days.

xxxviii. A certain brother was beset by lust. It befell that he came into a certain town of Egypt, and seeing the daughter of a priest of the pagans, he greatly loved her and said to her father, "Give her me to wife." But he answered him, "I cannot give her to thee, until I have asked my god." And going to the demon whom he worshipped, he said to him, "Behold, a certain monk has come to me, wishing to have my daughter; shall I give her to him?" And the demon made answer, "Ask him if he will deny his God, and his baptism, and his monk's vow."

And the priest came to him and said, "Deny thy God, and thy baptism, and thy monk's vow, and I shall give thee my daughter." He indeed consented. And straightway he saw as it might be a dove come out of his mouth and fly into heaven. Then the priest came again to the demon and said, "He hath promised to

do these three things." And the devil answering said, "Thou shalt not give him thy daughter to wife, for his God hath not departed from him, but doth yet stand by him." And the priest coming to him said to the brother, "I cannot give her to thee, for thy God doth yet stand by thee, and hath not departed from thee." And the brother hearing this said within himself, "If God showeth me such kindness, when I did miserably deny Himself, and my baptism, and my monk's vow; if my good God doth stand by me in my wickedness, even now, why should I go from Him?" And returning to himself, he recovered his sober mind and came to the desert to a certain great old man, and told him what had come to pass. And the old man answered and said, "Sit with me in the cave, and fast for three weeks, and I shall plead with God for thee."

And the old man toiled for his brother, and pleaded with God, saying, "I pray thee, Lord, give me this soul, and accept his repentance." And God heard his prayer. And when the first week was ended, the old man came to that brother and asked him, saying, "Hast thou seen aught?" And the brother answered, "Yes: I saw a dove at the height of heaven, standing high above my head." And the old man said, "Look to thyself, and be thou intent upon God in thy prayer." At the end of the second week the old man came again to the brother and questioned him, saying, "Hast thou seen aught?" An he answered, "I saw the dove coming nigh my head." And the old man counselled him, saying, "Be very sober in mind, and pray." And when the third week was ended, again came the old man and asked him, saying, "Hast thou seen aught else?" And he answered, "I saw the dove, and it came and stood above my head, and I stretched out my hand to take it; but it rose and entered into my mouth." And the old man thanked God and said to the brother: "Behold, God hath accepted thy repentance: for the rest, look to thyself

and watch." And the brother answering said, "Behold, I shall abide with thee from this time forward until I die."

BOOK VI

That a Monk Ought Not to Possess Anything

ii. The abbot Daniel told the abbot Arsenius that at one time a magistrate came to him bringing him the will of a certain senator, a kinsman, who had left him a very great property. And taking the will, he made to tear it across: but the magistrate fell at his feet saying, "I pray thee, tear it not, for the blame will fall on my head." And the abbot Arsenius said to him, "I died before he did. And now that he is dead, how can he make me his heir?" And he sent back the will, accepting nothing.

iii. At one time the abbot Arsenius fell sick in Scete, and in his necessity he was in want even of a single penny. And when he could not find one, he accepted it from someone as alms, and said, "I thank Thee, Lord, that Thou hast made me worthy for Thy sake to come to this, that I in want must ask an alms."

vi. The abbot Theodore of Pherme had three fine codices. And he came to the abbot Macarius and said to him, "I have three codices, and I profit by the reading of them. And the brethren also come seeking to read them, and they themselves profit. Tell me, therefore, what I ought to do?" And the old man answering said, "These are good deeds: but better than all is to possess nothing." And hearing this, he went away and sold the aforenamed codices, and gave the price of them to the needy.

x. The abbot Cassian said that a certain Syncleticus had renounced the world and divided his substance among the poor, yet kept somewhat for his own use, for he had not the perfect will to humble himself by renouncing all things and to follow the rule of the common life of the brethren. And to him did Basil of holy memory say this word: "Thou hast ceased from the Senator, but hast not put on the monk."

xi. A brother said to the abbot Pisteramon, "What shall I do, for it is hard for me to sell what I have wrought with my own hands." And he answering said, "The abbot Sisois and the rest used to sell the work of their hands: there is no hurt in this. But when thou art selling, say at once the price of the goods that thou dost offer. And if thou dost wish to lower the price a little, that is for thee to say; and so thou shalt find quiet." And again the brother said, "If I have enough for my needs from elsewhere, dost think that I need not trouble about working with my hands?" The old man answering said, "Whatever thou hast, neglect not to work, and do as much as thou canst, but without perturbation of spirit."

xii. A brother asked the abbot Serapion, saying, "Say one word to me." The old man said, "What I have to say to thee is that thou hast taken the portion of the widow and the fatherless and set it in the window." For he had seen it full of codices.

xiii. It was asked of Syncletica of blessed memory if to have nothing is a perfect good. And she said, "It is a great good for those who are able. For those who can endure it endure suffering in the flesh, but they have quiet of soul. Even as stout garments trodden underfoot and turned over in the washing are made clean and white, so is a strong soul made steadfast by voluntary poverty."

xiv. Said the abbot Hyperichius, "The treasure house of the monk is voluntary poverty. Wherefore, my brother, lay up thy treasure in heaven: for there abide the ages of quiet without end."

xix. There came a certain unknown great one into Scete,

bringing with him gold, and he asked a priest in the desert to disburse it among the brethren. But the priest said to him, "The brethren have no need of it." And since he was exceeding urgent and would not be satisfied, he laid the basket with the coins at the doorway of the church, and the priest said, "Whoso hath need, let him take it." And no one touched it, or indeed so much as looked upon the gold. And the old man said to him, "God hath accepted thine offering: go, and give it to the poor." And he went away much edified.

xx. One brought an old man money, saying, "Take this for thy spending, for thou hast grown old and thou art ill." He was indeed a leper. But the old man said, "Dost thou come to take away my Shepherd after sixty years? Behold for all this long time of my infirmity, I have lacked for nothing, God supplying me and feeding me." And he would not consent to take it.

xxii. A brother asked a certain old man, saying, "Wouldst thou have me keep two gold pieces for myself against some infirmity of the body?" The old man, seeing his thought, that he was wishful to keep them, said, "Even so." And the brother going into his cell was torn by his thoughts, saying, "Thinkest thou, did the old man tell me the truth or no?" And rising up he came again to the old man, in penitence, and asked him, "For God's sake tell me the truth, for I am tormented thinking on these two gold pieces." The old man said to him, "I saw that thy will was set on keeping them. So I bade thee keep them: but indeed it its not good to keep more than the body's need. If thou hadst kept the two gold pieces, in them would have been thy hope. And if it should happen that they were lost, how should God have any thought for us? Let us cast our thoughts upon God: since it is for Him to care for us."

BOOK VII
Of Patience or Fortitude

i. When the holy abbot Antony was living in the desert, his soul fell into a weariness and confusion of thought, and he began saying to God, "Lord, I would be made whole and my thoughts will not suffer me. What shall I do in this tribulation, how shall I be whole?" And in a little while, rising up, he began to walk in the open, and he saw someone, as it might be himself, sitting and working: and then rising from his work and praying: and again sitting down and making a plait of palm-leaves, and then rising once again to prayer. Now it was an angel of the Lord sent to the reproof and warning of Antony. And he heard the voice of the angel, saying, "This do, and thou shalt be whole." And hearing it, he took great joy of it and courage. And in so doing, he found the deliverance that he sought.

iii. The abbot Ammonas said that he had spent fourteen years in Scete, entreating the Lord day and night, that He would give him power to master anger.

v. A certain brother who lived solitary was disturbed in mind, and making his way to the abbot Theodore of Pherme he told him that he was troubled. The old man said to him, "Go, humble thy spirit and submit thyself, and live with other men." So he went away to the mountain, and dwelt with others. And afterwards he came back to the old man and said to him, "Nor in living with other men have I found peace." And the old man said, "If thou canst not be at peace in solitude, nor yet with men, why didst thou will to be a monk? Was it not that thou shouldst have tribulation? Tell me now, how many years hast thou been in this habit?" And the brother said, "Eight." And the old man said, "Believe me, I have been in this habit seventy years, and not for one day could I find peace: and thou wouldst have peace in eight?"

xxii. A certain old man told this tale: A certain brother was in a cell, and trial came upon him: if any saw him, they would not greet him, nor receive him into their cell: if he had need of bread, no one would lend to him: and if he came from harvesting, no one would invite him in to refresh himself, as is the custom. So he came by himself from harvest through the heat, and he had no loaves in his cell: and in all these things he gave God thanks. And God, seeing his patience, took this struggle and trial from him. And lo! one suddenly knocked at the door, leading a camel laden with bread out of Egypt; and when he saw it, the brother began to weep, saying, "Lord, I am not worthy of even a little tribulation." And when his trial was thus past, his brethren had him into their cells, and into the church, and made much of him.

xxvi. An old man said, "The ancients did not readily remove from place to place unless it might be for three things: that is, if there was any who had a grudge against him, and he could not pacify him do what he would: or again if it befell that he were praised by many: or if he ran into temptation of fornication."

xxvii. A certain brother said to the abbot Arsenius, "What shall I do, Father, for I am harried by my thoughts that say to me, 'Thou canst not fast, nor toil, nor visit the sick, and in these things profit is'?" The old man, seeing the devil's sowing, said to him, "Go—eat and drink and sleep, so long as thou dost not go out of thy cell, knowing that perseverance in his cell brings the monk to his calling." Now when he had spent three days he was weary exceedingly, and he found a few palm-leaves and split them, and again on the morrow he began to make them into a plait. And when he grew hungry, he said to himself, "Here are a few more palm-leaves, I shall spread them out, and then I shall eat." And when he had finished with them, he said again, "I shall read a little, and then eat." And when he had read a little, he said, "I shall say a few psalms, and then I shall eat with a good conscience." And so little by little, God working with him, he progressed, till he came to his calling. And when he had learned confidence against evil thoughts, he conquered them.

xxxi. A certain old man dwelt in the desert, and his cell was far from water, about seven miles: and once when he was going to draw water, he flagged and said to himself, "What need is there for me to endure this toil? I shall come and live near the water." And saying this, he turned about and saw one following him and counting his footprints: and he questioned him, saying, "Who art thou?" And he said, "I am the angel of the Lord, and I am sent to count thy footprints and give thee thy reward." And when he heard him, the old man's heart was stout, and himself more ready, and he set his cell still farther from that water.

xxxii. The Fathers used to say, "If temptation befall thee in the place thou dost inhabit, desert not the place in the time of temptation: for if thou dost, wheresoever thou goest, thou shalt find what thou fliest before thee."

xxxiii. A certain brother while he was in the community was restless and frequently moved to wrath. And he said within himself, "I shall go and live in some place in solitude: and when I have no one to speak to or to hear, I shall be at peace and this passion of anger will be stilled." So he went forth and lived by himself in a cave. One day he filled a jug for himself with water and set it on the ground, but it happened that it suddenly overturned. He filled it a second time, and again it overturned: and he filled it a third time and set it down, and it overturned again.

And in a rage he caught up the jug and broke it. Then when he had come to himself, he thought how he had been tricked by the spirit of anger and said, "Behold, here am I alone, and nevertheless he hath conquered me. I shall return to the community, for in all places there is need for struggle and for patience and above all for the help of God." And he arose and returned to his place.

xxxiv. A brother asked an old man, saying, "What shall I do, Father, for I do nothing a monk should, but in a kind of heedlessness I am eating and drinking and sleeping and always full of bad thoughts and great perturbation, going from one task to another, and from one thought to another?" And the old man said, "Sit thou in thy cell, and do what thou canst, and be not troubled: for the little that thou dost now is even as when Antony did great things and many in the desert. For I have this trust in Go, that whoever sits in his cell for His name and keeps his conscience shall himself be found in Antony's place."

xxxvi. An old man said, "Even as a tree cannot bear fruit if it be often transplanted, no more can a monk that is often removing from one place to another."

xxxvii. A certain brother who was tormented by his thoughts urging him to leave the monastery, told it to the abbot. And he said, "Go, and sit down, and give thy body in pledge to the wall of thy cell, and go not out thence: but let thy thought go: let it think as much as it likes, provided thou fling not thy body out of the cell."

xxxviii. An old man said, "The cell of the monk is the furnace in Babylon, where the three young men found the Son of God: and it is also the pillar of cloud from which God spoke to Moses."

xliv. At one time an old man who lived the solitary life fell ill: and as he had no one to tend him, he would rise and eat whatever he could find in his cell: and the days passed and no one came to visit him. But when thirty days had gone by and no one came, the Lord sent His angel, and he ministered unto him. So it was for seven days, and then the fathers remembered and said one to another, "Let us go and see if perchance that old man is ill." But when they came and knocked, the angel departed from him. And the old man called out from within, "Go hence, my brethren." But they lifted the door from its hinge and entered in and asked him why he had called out. And he said, "For thirty days I travailed in my infirmity, and no one visited me, and lo! it is now seven days since the Lord sent His angel to minister unto me, and when ye came, he departed from me." And saying these words he slept in peace. But the brethren marvelled and glorified God, saying, "The Lord doth not leave them that hope in Him desolate."

BOOK VIII
That Nothing Ought to Be Done for Show

iv. A certain Eulogius was disciple of John the archbishop: this Eulogius was a priest and abstemious, and fasted two days at a time, and sometimes would prolong his fast for a week, and would eat naught but bread and salt; and for this he had praise of men. He came to the abbot Joseph in the place that is called Panephus, believing that he would find still harsher abstinence with him. And the old man welcomed him with joy, and for love's sake made ready for him whatever he had. But the disciples of Eulogius said, "The priest eats nothing but bread and salt," so the abbot Joseph began to eat in silence. And when they had spent three days thus, and heard no sound of psalm or prayer (for the office was said in secret), they went away nothing edified. But by the ordering of God a mist came down, and they wandered from the road and came back to the old man: and before they knocked at the door, they heard chanting: they waited for a long time listening, and then knocked, and again the old man welcomed them joyfully. Now those who were with Eulogius, it being hot, took up a vessel and gave it to him to drink: but it was river-water mixed with sea-water and he could not drink it. And turning over these things in his mind, he began to question the old man to learn from him his way of life, saying, "How is it, Father, that at first ye did not chant, but did begin as soon as we went out, and that when I would have drunk water, I found it salt?" And the old man said, "Some brother hath been upset, and by mistake hath mixed sea-water with it." But Eulogius went on questioning the old man, desirous to know the truth. And the old man said to him, "This little chalice of wine is that which love provides, and this is for the water which the brethren regularly drink." And by these words he taught him to have discrimination in his thoughts, and purged him of all that hath power to move the mind after the manner of men: and he became familiar with all men, and thereafter would eat whatever was set before him. He learned moreover himself to labour in secret, and he said to the old man, "Verily, thine is the labour of love."

vi. At one time there came a certain brother to the abbot Theodore of Pherme and spent three days questioning him that he might hear some word from him. But he did not answer him, and he went away sad. Then said his disciple, "Father, wherefore didst not thou talk with him, for behold he is gone away sad?" And the old man said, "Believe me, if I had no speech with him, it is that he is a pedlar that would prank himself in another man's words."

vii. Another brother asked the abbot Theodore, saying, "Wilt thou that for some days I eat no bread?" And the old man said, "Thou dost well, and I myself have done the like." And the brother said to him, "I would like to take some peas to the mill and make flour of them." And the abbot Theodore said to him, "If thou art already for the mill, make thyself bread: and what need is there of this quibbling?"

viii. Another brother questioned the same old man, the abbot Theodore, and began to discuss and inquire into labours which he had not yet performed. And the old man said to him, "Thou hast not yet found thy ship, nor put thy baggage in her, nor begun to sail, and art thou already in the city whither thou hast planned to come? When thou hast first laboured in that whereof thou speakest, then speak from out the thing itself."

ix. The abbot Cassian said there came a certain brother to the abbot Serapion, and the old man urged him to make the accustomed prayer: but he, declaring that he was a sinful man and unworthy of the monk's habit that he wore, would not consent. The old man would have washed his feet, and again using the same words, he would in no way consent. The old man however, made him eat, and began in love to counsel him, saying, "My son, if thou dost wish to profit, stay in thy cell and look to thyself and the work of thine hands: for it will advantage thee less to travel than to sit still." But on hearing this, he was angered and his countenance altered and he could not hide it from the old man. So the abbot Serapion said to him, "But now thou wert saying, 'I am a sinful man,' and accusing thyself as unfit even to live: and because I gave thee loving counsel, oughtst thou to grow so angry? If thou wouldst in truth be humble, learn to bear manfully such things as are put upon thee by another, and do not thou pour baleful words over thyself." And the brother hearing this did penance before the old man and went much profited away.

x. At one time a provincial judge heard of the abbot Moses and set out into Scete to see him: but the old man heard of his coming and got up to flee into the marsh. And the judge with his following met him, and questioned him, saying, "Tell me, old man, where is the cell of the abbot Moses?" And he said, "Why would ye seek him out? The man is a fool and a heretic." So the judge coming to the church said to the clergy, "I had heard of the abbot Moses and came to see him: but lo! we met an old man journeying into Egypt, and asked him where might be the cell of the abbot Moses, and he said, 'Why do you seek him? He is a fool and a heretic.'" The clergy, on hearing this, were perturbed and said, "What was this old man like, who spoke thus to you of the holy man?" And they said, "He was an old man wearing a very ancient garment, tall and black." And they said, "It is the abbot himself: and because he did not wish to be seen by you, he told you these things about himself." And mightily edified, the judge went away.

xi. A brother asked the abbot Mathois, saying, "If I go to live in a certain place, how wouldst thou have me behave there?" The old man said to him, "If thou dost dwell in a place, seek not to make thyself a name for this or that, saying, 'I do not come into the assembly of the brethren,' or 'I do not eat this or that,' for these things make thee an empty name, but thereafter thou shalt suffer annoyance, for when men hear of such, thither they run."

xii. The abbot Nisteron the elder was walking in the desert with a certain brother and seeing a dragon they fled. And the brother said to him, "Art thou also afraid, Father?" The old man replied, "I am not afraid, my son: but it was expedient that

I should flee at sight of the dragon, that I might not have to fly the spirit of vainglory."

xvii. At one time the judge of the province came to see the abbot Simon, and he took the leather girdle that he wore and climbed into the palm-tree to prune it. And when they came up they said to him, "Where is the old man who inhabits this solitude?" And he answered, "There is no solitary here." And when he had thus spoken the judge departed.

xviii. Another time another judge came to see him [Simon] and the clergy that went before him said to him, "Father, make thyself ready, for the judge hath heard of thee and comes for thy blessing." And he said, "I will indeed make myself ready." And he covered himself with his sackcloth, and taking in his hand bread and cheese, sat down at the doorway of his cell and began to eat. In due course the judge came with his escort, and at the sight they made a scorn of him, saying, "Is this the solitary monk of whom we have heard such great things?" And straightway they turned about, and departed to their own place.

xix. The holy Syncletica said, "A treasure that is known is quickly spent: and even so any virtue that is commented on and made a public show of is destroyed. Even as wax is melted before the face of fire, so is the soul enfeebled by praise, and loses the toughness of its virtues."

xxii. There was a certain one that abstained from food and ate no bread: he came to one of the Fathers. By chance there came also other pilgrims, and the old man made them a little broth. And when they sat down to eat, the abstemious brother set down for himself a pea that he had steeped, and chewed it. And when they got up from the table, the old man took him aside and said to him, "Brother, if thou comest to any one, do not show off to him thy way of life: if thou dost wish to keep to thine own way, abide in thy cell and go nowhere out from it." And he accepted the words of the old man, and made himself thereafter share the common life in whatsoever fell to his lot with the brethren.

BOOK IX

That One Ought Not to Judge Any Man

i. It happened that temptation fell upon a brother in the monastery of abbot Elias, and they cast him out: and he came to the mountain, to abbot Antony. After he had been with him for some time, Antony sent him back to the community whence he had come out. But when they saw him, they again drove him away: and again he made his way to the abbot Antony, saying, "They would not receive me, Father." Then the old man sent to them, saying, "A ship was wrecked at sea, and lost all the cargo that it carried, and with hard toil was the empty ship brought at last to land. Is it your wish to sink on land the ship that hath come safe from sea?" And they recognised that it was the abbot Antony who had sent him back and straightway they took him in.

ii. A certain brother had sinned, and the priest commanded him to go out from the church. But Bessarion rose up and went out with him, saying, "I too am a sinful man."

iv. Once a brother in Scete was found guilty, and the older brethren came in assembly and sent to the abbot Moses, asking him to come: but he would not. Then the priest sent to him, saying: "Come: for the assembly of brethren awaits thee." And he rose up and came. But taking with him a very old basket, he filled it with sand and carried it behind him. And they went out to meet him, asking, "Father, what is this?" And the old man said to them, "My sins are running behind me and I do not see them, and I am come today to judge the sins of another man." And they heard him, and said naught to the brother, but forgave him.

vi. A brother asked the abbot Pastor, saying, "If I should see my brother's fault, is it good to hide it?" The old man said to him, "In what hour we do cover up our brother's sins, God shall cover ours: and in what hour we do betray our brother's shames, in like manner God shall betray our own."

x. An old man said, "Judge not him who is guilty of fornication, if thou art chaste: or thou thyself wilt offend a similar law. For He who said, 'Thou shall not fornicate' said also 'Thou shalt not judge.'"

xii. There were two brethren of good life in the community, and they had so attained that either saw the grace of God in the other. But it came to pass that one of them went out of the monastery on a Friday and saw one eating in the morning. And he said to him, "Dost thou eat at this hour on a Friday?" On the following day there was the wonted celebration of mass; and his brother, looking upon him, saw that the grace given him had departed from him; and he was saddened. When he had come into the cell, he said to him, "What hast thou done, brother, that I do not see, as before, the grace of God in thee?" He answered and said, "Neither in act nor in thought am I conscious of any evil." His brother said to him, "Hast thou spoken a harsh word to any one?" And he, remembering, said, "Yea. Yesterday I saw someone eating in the morning and I said to him: 'Dost thou eat at this hour on a Friday?' This is my sin: but travail with me for two weeks, and let us ask God to forgive me." They did so: and after two weeks the brother saw the grace of God again coming upon his brother, and they were comforted, giving thanks to God, who alone is good.

BOOK X
Of Discretion

i. The abbot Antony said, "There be some that wear out their bodies with abstinence: but because they have no discretion, they be a great way from God."

vii. The abbot Marcus asked the abbot Arsenius, saying, "Is it good to have no kind of solace in one's cell? For I saw a brother that had a few green herbs about his cell, and he was rooting them out." And the abbot Arsenius said, "It is indeed good: but every man must act according to his own powers: if that brother should not be able to endure that kind of virtue, let him plant them again."

xiii. The abbot Agatho said, "If an angry man were to raise the dead, because of his anger he would not please God."

xiv. There came three old men to the abbot Achilles: and one of them was ill spoken of. And one of the three said to the abbot, "Father, make me a fishing-net"; but he refused. And the second said, "Make it for us, so that we may have something to remember thee by in our monastery." And he said, "I have not time." Then the third, he that was ill spoken of, said to him, "Make me a net, so that I may have a blessing from thine own hands, Father." And he straightway answered him, "I shall make it for thee."

Then the first two who he had refused asked him privately, "How was it that thou wouldst not make it for us when we asked thee, and yet saidst to this man, 'I shall make it for thee'?"

And the old man made answer, "I said to you, 'I shall not do it, because I have not time,' and ye were not grieved: but if I did not do it for this man, he would say, 'The old man has heard about me, that I have an ill name, and for this reason he would not make the net': and I straightway set to upon the cord to soothe his spirit, lest he should be swallowed up of sadness."

xv. They told of a certain old man that he had lived fifty years neither eating bread nor readily drinking water: and that he said, "I have killed in me lust and avarice and vainglory." The abbot Abraham heard that he said these things, and he came to him and said, "Hast thou spoken thus?" And he answered, "Even so." And the abbot Abraham said, "Behold, thou dost enter thy cell, and find upon thy bed a woman: canst thou refrain from thinking that it is a woman?" And he said, "No: but I fight my thoughts, so as not to touch that woman." And the abbot Abraham said, "So then, thou hast not slain lust, for the passion itself liveth, but it is bound. Again if thou art walking on the road and seest stones and potsherds, and lying amongst them gold, canst thou think of it but as stones?" And he answered, "No: but I resist my thought, so as not to pick it up." And the abbot Abraham said "So then, passion liveth: but it is bound." And again the abbot Abraham said, "If thou shouldst hear of two brethren, that one loves thee and speaks well of thee, but the other hates thee and disparages thee, and they should come to thee, wouldst thou give them an equal welcome?" And he said, "No: but I should wrest my mind so that I should do as much for him that hated me as for him that loved me." And the abbot Abraham said, "So then these passions live, but by holy men they are in some sort bound."

xvi. One of the Fathers told how a certain old man was ever diligently toiling in his cell, and clothed himself in a mat: and when he sought out the abbot Ammon, the abbot Ammon saw him wearing his mat, and said to him "This profits thee nothing." And the old man said to him, "Three thoughts harry me: one, that would compel me to withdraw myself elsewhere in the desert; another, that I should seek a strange land where no one knows me; and a third, that I should shut myself up in my cell so as to see no man, and eat only every third day." And the abbot Ammon said to him, "None of these three things would profit thee to do: but do thou sit in thy cell, and eat a little every day, and have ever in thy heart the saying of the publican that is read in the Gospel, and so thou shalt be saved."

xvii. The abbot Daniel used to say, "Even as the body flourisheth, so doth the soul become withered: and when the body is withered, then doth the soul put forth leaves." Again he said, "Insomuch as the body is cherished, so doth the soul wax lean: and when the body hath grown lean, then does the soul wax fat."

xviii. The abbot Daniel also told how when the abbot Arsenius was in Scete, there was a certain monk that pilfered such things as the old men had: but the abbot Arsenius, desiring to do him a kindness and give the old men peace, brought him into his cell and said to him, "Whatever thou wouldst have I shall give thee, if thou wilt but cease to steal": and he gave him gold and money and garments, and all that he had in his wallet he gave him. But he began to steal again. And the old men, seeing that he would not be at peace, cast him out, saying "If it should happen that a brother hath some infirmity of his body, we must support him: but if he hath stolen and will not cease for admonishing, send him away: for he doth harm to his own soul, and troubleth all that dwell in the place."

xxv. At one time there came one of the fathers to the abbot Theodore, and said to him, "Behold, such and such a brother has gone back to the world." And the abbot Theodore said to him, "Marvel not at that: but when thou hearest that any one hath prevailed to escape from the jaws of the Enemy, then mayst thou marvel."

xxvii. They used to tell of the abbot John of short stature that he once said to his elder brother, "I would fain be secure as the angels are secure, toiling not, but serving God without stay," and stripping himself of his garments, he went into the desert. And when a week had been spent there, he returned to his brother: and while he was knocking at the door, his brother answered before he would open, saying, "Who are thou?" And he said, "I am John." And his brother answered and said to him, "John is become an angel and is no longer among men." However, he went on knocking, saying, "I am he." And he would not open to him, but sent him away in distress. Then afterwards opening the door he said to him, "If thou art a man, thou must needs work again, so as to live: if however thou art an angel, why dost thou ask to come into the cell?" And he did penance, saying, "Forgive me, brother, for I have sinned."

xxxiii. The abbot Longinus asked the abbot Lucius saying, "I meditate three things: first, that I shall go on pilgrimage." And the old man answered him, "If thou dost not hold thy tongue wheresoever thou goest, thou shalt be no pilgrim. But control thy tongue here, and here shalt thou be a pilgrim." And the abbot Longinus said to him, "Another plan have I, that I shall fast two days at a time." And the abbot Lucius replied, "Isaiah the prophet said, *If thou wouldst bow down thy head like a bulrush, not thus would thy fast be accepted,* but rather refrain thy mind from evil thoughts." And the abbot Longinus said, "The third thing that is in my mind, is to refuse the sight of men." And the abbot Lucius answered him, "Unless thou shalt first amend thy life going to and fro amongst others, thou shalt not avail to amend it dwelling alone."

xxxiv. The abbot Macarius said, "If we dwell upon the harms that have been wrought on us by men, we amputate from our mind the power of dwelling upon God."

xxxvii. A brother asked the abbot Pastor, saying, "Trouble has come upon me and I would fain leave this place." And the old man said to him, "For what reason?" And he said, "I have heard tales of a certain brother that do not edify me." And the old man said, "Are the tales true that thou hast heard?" And he said, "Yea, Father, they are true: for the brother who told me is faithful." And he answering said, "He is not faithful that told thee: for if he were faithful, he would never tell thee such things: God heard tell of the men of Sodom, but He believed it not till He went down and saw with His own eyes." But he said, "And I have seen with mine own eyes." The old man heard him and looked upon the ground and picked up a little straw and said to him, "What is this?" And he answered, "A straw." And again the old man gazed at the roof of the cell and said, "What is this?" And he said, "It is the beam that holds up the roof." And the old man said to him, "Take it to thy heart that thy sins are as this beam: the sins of that brother of whom thou dost speak are as this poor straw."

xl. A brother asked the abbot Pastor, saying, "I have sinned a great sin, and I am willing to do penance for three years." But the abbot Pastor said, "That is a good deal." And the brother said, "Dost thou order me one year?" And again the old man said, "That is a good deal." Some who stood by said, "Up to forty days?" The old man said, "That is a good deal." And then he added, "I think that if a man would repent with his whole heart and would not reckon to do again that for which he now repents, God would accept a penance of three days."

xliv. The abbot Joseph asked the abbot Pastor, saying, "How should one fast?" And the abbot Pastor said, "I would have it so that every day one should deny one's self a little in eating, so as not to be satisfied." The abbot Joseph said to him, "But when thou wast a young man, didst thou not fast two days and upwards?" And the old man, "Two days, believe me, and three, and a week: but all these things did the great old men bring to proof: and they found that it is good to eat a little every day, and on certain days a little less: and they have shown us this master road, for it is easy and light."

xliv. The abbot Pastor said, "If a man has sinned and denies it not, but says 'I have sinned,' scold him not, for thou wilt break the purpose of his heart. But rather say to him, 'Be not sad, my brother, but watch thyself hereafter,' and thou wilt rouse his heart to repentance."

liii. He said again, "If there be three in one place, and one of them lives the life of holy quiet, and another is ill and gives thanks, and the third tends them with an honest heart, these three are alike, as if their work was one."

lv. A brother came to the abbot Pastor and said to him, "Many thoughts come into my mind, and I am in peril from them." And the old man pushed him out under the open sky, and said to him, "Expand thy chest and catch the wind." And he answered, "I cannot do it." And the old man said to him: "If thou canst not do this, neither canst thou prevent thoughts from entering in, but it is for thee to resist them."

lxxiii. At one time there came two old men from the parts about Pelusium, to the abbess Sara: and as they were walking they said one to the other, "Let us humble this old woman." And they said to her. "Look to it that thy spirit be not puffed up, and thou shouldst say, 'Behold, men that are anchorites come to me that am a woman.'" And the abbess Sara said to them, "A woman in sex, but not in spirit."

lxxvi. At one time there came from the city of Rome a monk that had had a great place in the palace, and he dwelt in Scete near by the church: and he had with him one servant that ministered unto him. And the priest of the church, seeing his infirmity and knowing that he was a man delicately nurtured, used to send him such things as the Lord gave him or were brought into the church. And when he had spent twenty-five years in Scete, he became a man of contemplation, of prophetic spirit and notable. And one of the great Egyptian monks, hearing of his fame, came to see him, hoping to find a more austere discipline with him. And when he had come in, he greeted him: and they prayed, and sat down. But the Egyptian, seeing him softly clad, and a bed of reeds and a skin spread under him and a little head-rest under his head, and his feet clean with sandals on them, was inwardly scandalised, because in that place it was not the custom so to live, but rather in stern abstinence. But the old Roman, having discernment and vision, perceived that the Egyptian was scandalised within himself, and said to his servant, "Make us good cheer today, for the sake of this Father who hath come." And he cooked a few vegetables that he had, and they rose up at the fitting time and did eat: he had also a little wine, by reason of his infirmity, and they drank it. And when evening was come, they said the twelve psalms, and slept: and in like fashion during the night. And rising in the morning the Egyptian said, "Pray for me." And he went away not edified.

And when he had gone a little way, the old Roman, desiring to heal his mind, sent after him and called him back. And when he had come, he again welcomed him joyfully, and questioned him, saying, "Of what province art thou?" And he answered, "I am an Egyptian." And he said to him, "Of what city?" And he answered, "I am of no city at all, nor have I ever dwelt in any city." And he said to him, "Before thou wert a monk, what didst thou do in the place where thou didst dwell?" And he answered, "I was a herd in the fields." And he said to him, "Where didst thou sleep?" And he answered, "In the field." And he said, "Hadst thou any coverlet?" And he answered, "What should I do with bedding sleeping in the fields?" And he said, "How didst thou sleep?" And he answered, "On the bare ground." And he said, "What didst thou eat in the field, and what kind of wine didst thou drink?" And he answered, "I ate dry bread, and any sort of salt fish if I could come by it, and I drank water." And the old man said, "It was hard toil." And he said, "Was there a bath on the estate where thou couldst wash thyself?" And he said, "Nay, but I used to wash in the river, when I wished to." And when the old man had drawn all this from his replies and understood the manner of his former life and his toil, being wishful to profit him he told him of his own past life when he was in the world, saying, "I, this poor man that you see, am of that great city, Rome, and held the highest place in the palace, beside the Emperor." And when the Egyptian heard him begin to speak, he was struck with compunction, and listened eagerly to hear what he would say. And he went on: "So then, I left Rome and came into this solitude." And again he said, "I whom you see, had great houses and much wealth, and despising them I came to this small cell." And again he said, "I, whom you see, had beds decked with gold and coverlets most precious: and for these God hath given me this mattress of papyrus and this skin. And my garments were costly beyond price, and for them I use these poor rags." Again he said, "On the keeping of my table, much gold was expended: and for this He gives me these few herbs and a small cup of wine. Many were the slaves who served me, and for these lo! God had put compassion in this one man's heart, to tend me. For a bath I pour a little water on my feet, and

I wear sandals because of my infirmity. And again for the pipe and lyre and other kinds of music wherein I delighted at my feasts, I say to myself twelve psalms by day, and twelve by night. But for those sins of mine that I then sinned, I offer now in quiet this poor and useless service unto God. Wherefore consider, Father, and be not scandalised because of my infirmity." And the Egyptian, hearing these things and turning upon himself said, "Sorrow upon me, that I out of much tribulation and heavy toil did rather come to rest and refreshing in the monastic life, and what I had not, I now have: but thou from great worldly delight art come of thine will into tribulation, and from high glory and riches art come into humility and poverty." And he went away mightily profited, and became his friend, and would often come to him to learn of him: for he was a man of discerning and filled with the fragrance of the Holy Ghost.

xciv. There came three brethren to a certain old man in Scete, and one of them asked him, saying, "Father, I have committed the Old and New Testaments to memory." And the old man answered and said, "Thou hast filled the air with words." And the second asked him, saying, "I have written the Old and New Testaments with my own hand." But he said to him, "And thou hast filled the windows with manuscripts." And the third said, "The grass grows on my hearthstone." And the old man answered and said, "And thou hast driven hospitality from thee."

c. An old man said, "If some aggravating discourse shall arise between thyself and another, and the other denies it, saying, 'I did not say that,' do not contend with him and say, 'Thou didst say it,' for he will be exasperated and say to thee, 'Good: I have said.'"

cx. A certain brother, having renounced the world and taken the habit, straightway shut himself up, saying, "I am minded to be a solitary." But when the older men of the neighbourhood heard it, they came and threw him out and made him go round the cells of the brethren and do penance before each, saying, "Forgive me, for I am no solitary, but have only now attempted to begin to be a monk."

cxi. Certain old men said, "If thou seest a young man ascending by his own will up to heaven catch him by the foot and throw him down upon earth, for it is not expedient for him."

cxiv. An old man said, "The prophets wrote books: then after them came our fathers, and wrought much upon them, and again their successors committed them to memory. But then came the generation that now is, and wrote them on papyrus and parchments, and laid them idle in the windows."

BOOK XI
That One Ought to Live Soberly

i. A brother asked the abbot Arsenius, that he might hear some word from him. And the old man said to him, "Whatever power thou hast, strive that the life which is within thee may be according to God, and may conquer the passions of the outer man." He said again, "If we seek God, He will appear to us: and if we hold Him, He will stay with us."

ii. The abbot Agatho said, "A monk ought not to have his conscience able to accuse him in aught whatsoever." Now when the aforesaid abbot Agatho was dying, he remained for three days motionless, holding his eyes open. And the brethren shook him, saying, "Father, where art thou?" And he answered, "I stand in sight of the divine Judgment." And they said, "Art thou afraid?" And he said, "Here I have toiled with what strength I had to keep the commandments of God: but I am a man, and I know not whether my works have been pleasing in His sight."

The brethren say to him, "And hast thou no confidence that thy works are according to God?" And the old man said, "I do not presume, until I have come before God: for the judgments of God are other than the judgments of men." And when they would have questioned him for further speech, he said to them, "Show me your love and speak not to me, for I am busy." And this said, straightway with joy he sent forth his spirit. For they saw him gathering his spirit together, as one who greets his dear friends. He had great guard in all things and used to say, that without watchfulness a man may climb to no virtue.

iv. The abbot Ammois said at the beginning to the abbot Arsenius, "How dost thou see me now?" And he said, "As an angel, Father." And a while after he asked him again, "Now how dost thou see me?" And he said, "As Satan, for even if thou art making good discourse, it is to me as a sword."

v. The abbot Allois said, "Unless a man shall say in his heart, 'I alone and God are in this world,' he shall not find quiet."

vi. He said again, "If a man willed it, in one day up till evening he might come at the measure of divinity."

viii. At one time the abbot Daniel and abbot Ammois were going on a journey together: and the abbot Ammois said, "When think you, Father, shall we be sitting in our cell?" The abbot Daniel said to him, "And who hath taken God from us? For now is God out of doors, and now is God in the cell."

xiv. It was said of the abbot John that he was once plaiting palm-leaves to make two baskets, and used them all in one basket, but knew it not till it reached the wall. For his mind was taken up with the contemplation of God.

xv. There was an old man in Scete who had indeed endurance of body, but not much heedfulness in remembering what was said to him. So he went to the abbot John the Short to consult him about forgetfulness: and after hearing his discourse, returned to his cell and forgot what the abbot John had said. Again he went and questioned him: but as soon as he reached his cell, he forgot what he had heard, and so, after much going to and fro, forgetfulness overmastered him. Some time after, meeting the abbot he said, "Father, dost thou know that I again forgot what thou didst say to me? But I did not come back, lest I should be a trouble to thee." The abbot John said: "Go, light the lamp." And he lit it. And he said, "Bring other lamps, and light them from this one." And he did so. And the abbot John said to the old man, "Is the lamp injured in aught, that thou has lit the others from it?" And he said, "Nay." "So neither is John injured, if all Scete should come to me, nor am I hindered from the love of God: come therefore when thou wilt, hesitating not at all." And so by the patience of them both, God freed the old man of forgetfulness: for that indeed was the business of them that dwelt in Scete, to give courage to those who were besieged by any passion and who struggled in travail with themselves that they might come to good.

xxviii. At one time when the abbot Silvanus was living in Mount Sinai, his disciple was desirous to go about his tasks and said to the old man, "Release the water, and water the garden." And as he went out to release the water he covered his face with his hood, so that he looked only at his feet. It befell that at that very hour a certain man came to visit him, and seeing him from a long way off, wondered what he might be doing. And when he came up with him, he said, "Tell me, Father, why didst thou cover thy face with thy hood, and so water the garden?" And the old man said, "Lest mine eyes should see the trees and my mind be taken up with looking upon them and cease from its task."

xxix. The abbot Moses asked the abbot Silvanus, saying, "Can a man every day make a beginning of the good life?" The abbot

Silvanus answered him, "If he be diligent, he can every day and every hour begin the good life anew."

xxx. Certain men once asked the abbot Silvanus, saying, "Under what discipline of life hast thou laboured to have come at this wisdom of thine?" And he answering, said, "Never have I suffered to remain in my heart a thought that angered me."

xxxii. The holy Syncletica said, "Let us live soberly, for through the senses of our body, even though it be against our will, thieves do enter in: for how shall the house not be darkened, if the smoke rising without shall find the windows open?"

xliii. A brother said to an old man, "I see no war in my heart." And the old man said to him, "Thou art like a chariot-gate, and whosoever will may enter and go and come where he pleases, and thou knowest not what is going on. But if thou hadst a door and wouldst shut it, nor suffer evil thoughts to come in by it, then wouldst thou see them standing without and warring against thee."

xliv. They told of a certain old man that when his thoughts said to him, "Let be today: thou shalt repent tomorrow," he would contradict them, saying, "Nay, but I shall repent today: tomorrow, may the will of God be done."

li. A certain brother was steeping palm-leaves in his cell: and when he sat down to weave the plaits, his thoughts said to him to go and visit a certain old man. And again he thought within himself and said, "I shall go in a few days." And again his imagination said to him, "If he should die meanwhile, what should I do? I shall go now and talk to him, because it is summer weather." And again he said to himself, "Now is not the time." And again he thought to himself, "But when thou art cutting bulrushes to make mats, that is the time." And again he said, "I shall spread out these palm-leaves and then I shall go." And again he said to himself, "But today is a fine day." And getting up he left the palm-leaves steeping and took his sheepskin and went off.

But there was an old man his near neighbour, a far-seeing man: and seeing him walking eagerly, he called out to him, "Prisoner, prisoner, whither art thou running? Come here to me." And when he had come, the old man said to him, "Go back to thy cell." And the brother told him the ebb and flow that had been in his thoughts, and so went back to his cell. And coming in, he fell upon his face and did penance. And when he had finished, there was a great shout of devils, saying, "Thou hast conquered, monk, thou hast conquered." And the mat on which he was lying was burnt as with fire, but the demons vanished like smoke: and so that brother learned their wiles.

BOOK XII

That One Ought to Pray Without Ceasing, and Soberly

i. They told of the abbot Arsenius that on Saturday evening with the Sabbath drawing on, he would leave the sun behind him and stretching out his hand towards heaven, would pray until with the morning of the Sabbath the rising sun shone upon his face: and so he would abide.

ii. The brethren asked the abbot Agatho, saying, "Father, which virtue in this way of life is most laborious?" And he said to them, "Forgive me, but to my mind there is no labour so great as praying to God: for when a man wishes to pray to his God, the hostile demons make haste to interrupt his prayer, knowing that their sole hindrance is in this, a prayer poured out to God. With any other labour that a man undertakes in the life of religion, however instant and close he keeps to it, he hath some rest: but prayer hath the travail of a mighty conflict to one's last breath."

viii. There came to the abbot Joseph the abbot Lot, and said to him, "Father, according to my strength I keep a modest rule of prayer and fasting and meditation and quiet, and according to my strength I purge my imagination: what more must I do?" The old man, rising, held up his hands against the sky, and his fingers became like ten torches of fire, and he said, "If thou wilt, thou shalt be made wholly a flame."

ix. There came to the abbot Lucius in Enna certain monks of the kind called Euchitae, that is, the Men of Prayer: and the old man asked them saying, "What kind of handiwork do ye do?" And they said, "We touch no kind of handiwork, but as the Apostle says, we pray without ceasing." The old man said to them, "So ye do not eat?" They said, "Yea, we eat." And the old man said, "Now while ye are eating, who prays for you?" And again he questioned them, saying, "Ye do not sleep?" And they said, "We sleep." And the old man said, "And while ye sleep, who prays for you?" And they could find no answer.

And he said to them, "Forgive me, my brethren, but behold ye do not do as ye have said: but I shall show you how working with my hands, I pray without ceasing. For I sit, by the help of God, steeping my few palm-leaves and from them I weave a mat, and I say, 'Have mercy upon me, O God, according to thy loving-kindness: according to the multitude of thy tender mercies blot out my transgressions.'" And he said to them, "Is this a prayer or no?" And they said to him, "Yea." And he said, "When I abide all the day working and praying with heart and mouth, I make sixteen denarii more or less, and out of them I leave two at the door, and I spend the rest on food. But whoso finds the two denarii prays for me while I eat and sleep: and so by God's grace there is fulfilled in me as the Scripture saith, 'Pray without ceasing.'"

x. They asked the abbot Macarius, saying, "How ought we to pray?" and the old man said, "There is no need of much speaking in prayer, but often stretch out thy hands and say, 'Lord, as Thou wilt and as Thou knowest, have mercy upon me.' But if there is war in thy soul, add, 'Help me.' And because He knoweth what we have need of, He showeth us His mercy."

BOOK XIII
That One Should Show Hospitality
and Mercy with Cheerfulness

ii. The abbot Cassian said, "We came from Palestine into Egypt, to one of the Fathers. And he showed us hospitality, and we said to him, "Wherefore, in welcoming the brethren dost thou not keep the rule of fasting, as they do in Palestine?" And he made answer, "Fasting is ever with me, but I cannot keep you ever here: and though fasting be indeed useful and necessary, it is a matter of our own choosing: but love in its fulness the law of God requires at our hands. So, receiving Christ in you, I must show you whatever things be of love, with all carefulness: but when I have sent you away, then may I take up again the rule of fasting. The children of the bridegroom do not fast while the bridegroom is with them, but when he is taken from them, then shall they fast; it is in their own power."

vii. A brother came to a certain solitary: and when he was going away from him, he said, "Forgive me, Father, for I have made thee break thy rule." He made answer and said, "My rule is to receive thee with hospitality and send thee away in peace."

xiv. One of the old men used to say, "There be some that do great good, and the devil sends parsimony into their souls over trifles, so that they lose the merit of all the rest. Once as I sat in Oxyrinchus with a certain priest who gave much alms, there came a widow asking him for a little barley. And he said to her, 'Go, bring a peck, and I shall measure it for thee.' And she brought it to him. But he, measuring it by hand, said to her, 'This is more than a peck,' and brought shame on her.

"And when the widow had gone away, I said, 'Father, didst thou lend the barley to that widow, or what?' And he said, 'Nay, but I gave it to her.' And I said to him 'Then, if thou wert giving so much free, how couldst thou be so scrupulous over a trifle, and bring the woman to shame?'"

BOOK XIV
Of Obedience

iv. They used to tell of John, who was disciple to the abbot Paul, that he was of great obedience. There was in a certain place a memorial monument, and in it lived a most evil lioness. The old man, seeing her dung about the place, said to John, "Go and take away that dung." And he said, "But what shall I do, Father, about the lioness?" And the old man smiling, said to him, "If she comes out at thee, bind her and bring her here." So the brother set out that evening, and behold the lioness came out upon him: but he, obeying the old man's word, made a rush at her, to take her. The lioness fled, and he following after, saying, "Wait, for my abbot told me to bind thee": and he held her and tied her.

The old man meantime sat waiting, and the time grew long, and he began to be sorely uneasy about him; when behold him coming slowly along, and the lioness at the end of a rope behind him. The old man was astounded at the sight: but wishful to keep him humble, he struck him, saying, "Blockhead, hast thou brought me that foolish dog?" And straightway the old man loosed her, and sent her home to her own place.

v. They told of the abbot Silvanus that he had a disciple in Scete named Marcus, and he was of a great obedience, and also a writer of the ancient script: and the old man loved him because of his obedience. He had also other eleven disciples, who were aggrieved that he loved him more than them. And when the old men in the neighbourhood heard that the abbot loved him more than the rest, they took it ill. So one day they came to him: and the abbot Silvanus took them with him and went out of his cell, and began to knock at the cells of his disciples, one by one, saying, "Brother, come, I have need of thee." And not one of them obeyed him. He came to Marcus' cell and knocked, saying, "Marcus." And when he heard the old man's voice he came straight outside, and the old man sent him on some errand. Then the abbot Silvanus said to the old men, "Where are the other brethren?" And he went into Marcus' cell, and found a quaternion of manuscript which he had that moment begun, and was making thereon the letter O. And on hearing the old man's voice, he had not stayed to sweep the pen full circle so as to finish and close the letter that was under his hand. And the old men said, "Truly, abbot, him whom thou lovest we love also, for God loveth him."

BOOK XV
Of Humility

i. The abbot Antony, being at a loss in his meditation on the depth of the judgments of God, prayed, saying, "Lord, how comes it that some die in so short space of life, and some live to the further side of decrepit old age: and wherefore are some in want, and others rich with various means of wealth, and how are the unrighteous rich and the righteous oppressed by poverty?" And a voice came to him saying, "Antony, turn thine eyes upon thyself: for these are the judgments of God, and the knowledge of them is not for thee."

iv. At one time there came old men to the abbot Antony, and the abbot Joseph was with them. And the abbot Antony, wishing to prove them, brought the discourse to the Holy Scriptures. And he began to question, beginning with the younger men, what this or that word might mean. And each made answer as best he could. But he said to them, "Ye have not found it yet." After them he said to the abbot Joseph, "What dost thou say this word might be?" He answered "I know not." And the abbot Antony said, "Verily the abbot Joseph alone hath found the road, who saith that he doth not know."

v. At one time evil spirits came about the abbot Arsenius as he sat in his cell, and they began to harry him: but there came up certain brethren who were wont to minister to him: and standing outside his cell they heard him crying to the Lord and saying, "Lord depart not from me, because I have done no good thing in Thy sight. But grant me this, Lord, in Thy tender mercy, to have at least the beginnings of right living."

vi. They said of the abbot Arsenius that when he was in the palace none wore finer garments than he: and when he was in holy living, none was so poorly clad.

vii. At one time the abbot Arsenius was taking counsel with an old man of Egypt about his thoughts: and another seeing him said, "Abbot Arsenius, how is it that thou who art so great a scholar in the Latin tongue and the Greek, dost take counsel of this countryman about thy thoughts?" And he answered, "I have indeed apprehended the learning of Greeks and the Latins, as this world goes: but the alphabet of this countryman I have not yet been able to learn."

viii. The old men said that one certain folk had given the brethren in Scete a few dried figs, and because they were paltry they sent none of them to the abbot Arsenius, lest he might feel himself insulted. But when he heard of it, he did not go out as usual to the celebration of the holy office with the brethren, saying, "Ye have excommunicated me, in that ye would not give me the present that the Lord sent to the brethren, because I was not worthy to receive it." And when they all heard it, they were moved by the humility of the old man, and the priest set out and took him some of the dried figs and brought him back happy to the congregation.

ix. When the abbot Arsenius was dying, his disciples were troubled, and he said to them, "The hour is not yet come: when it hath come, I shall tell you. But I shall have you to judgment before the judgment seat of Christ, if ye suffer any one to do aught with my body." And they said, "What then shall we do, for we know not how to shroud or bury the dead?" And the old man said, "Know ye not to put a rope about my feet, and drag me to the mountain?"[19]

x. The abbot Daniel told of the abbot Arsenius that he would never willingly speak on any question of the Scriptures, which he could have done surpassing well had he willed, nor was he quick to write a letter to any. And when, after some time, he would come to the assembly of the brethren, he would sit behind a pillar, that no one might see his face, and lest he should gaze on any. He was of an angelic countenance, even as Jacob, with comely white hair, elegant in body, yet dry. He had a flowing beard, reaching to his middle: the lashes of his eyes had fallen with much weeping: he was a tall man, but bent with great age. He died aged ninety-five years. He had lived forty years in the palace of the Emperor Theodosius the elder, of blessed memory, who was father of Arcadius and Honorius, and he lived in Scete forty years, and in the place called Troe above Babylon, over against Memphis, ten years, and three years in Canopus of Alexandria: another two years he lived, returning again to Troe, and finished his course in peace and the fear of God, for he was a good man and full of the Holy Ghost and of faith.

xvi. The abbot Serapion said, "I have given myself far more travail of body than my son Zachary, and I have not come to the stature of his humility and his silence."

xviii. The abbot Pastor said that when brother Zachary was dying, the abbot Moses asked him, saying, "What seest thou?" And he answered, "Naught better, Father, than to hold one's peace." And he said, "It is true, my son: hold thy peace."

xix. Theophilus, bishop of Alexandria, of good memory, came at one time to Mount Nitria, and the abbot of that Mount came to him and the bishop said to him, "What further hast thou found on this road, Father?" And the old man said, "To blame and reproach myself without ceasing." And the bishop said to him, "There is no other road to follow, only this."

xxvii. At one time the abbot Mathois set out from Raythum into the parts of Gebalon: his brother also was with him. And the bishop of that place came to the aforesaid old man and made him a priest. And while they sat at meat together, the bishop said, "Forgive me, Father, for I know that this was against thy will: but I did presume to do it, that I might have thy blessing." But the old man said to him humbly, "And my heart did a little desire it: nevertheless I am heavy, because now must I be separated from my brother who is with me. And I cannot by myself fill up the number of the prayers that we used to pray together." And the bishop said, "If thou knowest that he is worthy, I shall ordain him also." And the abbot Mathois said, "Indeed, whether he be worthy I know not, but one thing I know, that he is more worthy than I." So the bishop ordained him also: and when they both departed from his life, they had never drawn near the altar to offer the Host. For the old man said, "I trust in God, that it may be He will not judge me hardly for my accepting of ordination, so long as I do not presume to consecrate the Host: for this is their office, who live without reproach."

xxviii. The abbot Mathois said, "The nearer a man approaches to God, the greater sinner he sees himself to be. For the prophet Isaiah saw God, and said that he was unclean and undone."

xxxvi. A brother asked the abbot Alonius, "What is contempt?" And the old man said, "To be below the creatures that have no reason, and to know that they are not condemned."

xlvii. A brother asked abbot Sisois, saying, "I know this of myself, that my mind is intent upon God." And the old man said to him, "It is no great matter that thy mind should be with God: but if thou didst see thyself less than any of His creatures, that were something."

lxv. There came certain folk to an old man in the Thebaid, bringing with them one vexed by a devil, that the old man might heal him. And after much pleading, the old man said to the devil, "Go out from this that God made." And the devil made answer: "I go, but I ask thee one question, and do thou answer me: who be the goats, and who the lambs?" And the old man said, "The goats indeed be such as I: but who the lambs may be, God knows." And hearing it, the devil cried out with a great voice, "Behold, because of this humbleness of thine, I go." And he went out that same hour.

lxviii. The devil appeared to a certain brother, transformed into an angel of light, and said to him, "I am the angel Gabriel and I am sent unto thee." But he said, "Look to it that thou wast not set to some other: for I am not worthy that an angel should be sent to me." And the devil was no more seen.

lxxii. They told of another old man that he persevered for seventy weeks fasting, eating but once a week. He inquired of God concerning a certain saying in Holy Writ, and God did not reveal it to him. Then he said within himself, "Behold, I have taken so great pains, and am profited nothing: I shall go to my brother, and enquire of him." So he went out, and as he was closing his door behind him, there came to him an angel from God, saying, "The seventy weeks of thy fasting brought thee not near to God: but now that thou art so humbled as to seek out thy brother, I am sent to expound to thee that saying." And he opened that Scripture which had perplexed him, and so departed from him.

BOOK XVI
Of Patience

i. The brethren used to tell of the abbot Gelasius that he had a codex in parchment worth eighteen solidi. It contained the whole of the Old and New Testaments: and the codex was placed in the Church, so that any of the brethren who willed might read it. But a certain brother, a stranger, arrived and joined himself to the old man, and seeing the codex he coveted it and stole it, and came out and went away. But the old man did not follow after him to lay hold on him, although he knew what he had done. Meantime the other made his way to the city, and sought about for a buyer. And when he had found one willing to buy it, he began to put the price at sixteen solidi. But the purchaser, wishing to judge of it, said, "Give it to me first that I may show it: and then I shall give you the price." So he gave him the codex to show. Then he who wished to buy it took it, and carried it to the abbot Gelasius to find out if it were a good codex and worth so much: for he told him the amount the seller was asking. And the old man said, "Buy it, for it is a good codex and worth the price that he said to you." But coming back, the buyer said otherwise to the seller, and not as he had heard from the old man: he said, "Behold, I showed it to the abbot Gelasius, and he told me that it was dear and not worth as much as thou didst say." On hearing this, the brother said, "Did he say naught else to thee?" And he answered, "Naught." Then the brother said, "I have no mind to sell this codex." And full of compunction he came to the old man, in penitence, and asked him to take back the codex: but the old man would not take it. Then the brother said to him, "If thou dost not take it, I shall never know quiet." And the old man said to him, "If thou canst have no quiet unless I take it, I shall take it." And the brother remained with him until he died, profiting by the patience of the old man.

xiii. There once came thieves into an old man's cell, and said to him, "Whatever thou hast in thy cell, we have come to take away." And he said, "Take whatever you see, my sons." So they took whatever they could find in the cell, and went away. But they forgot a little bag that was hidden in the cell. So the old man, picking it up, followed after them, shouting and saying, "My sons, ye forgot this: take it." But they, marvelling at the patience of the old man, brought everything back into his cell, and they all did penance, saying one to another, "Truly, this is a man of God."

xviii. There was once an old man given to wine, and he would finish a mat in one day, and sell it in the neighbouring town, and drink whatever he was paid for it. But late there came to him a certain brother, who lived with him and likewise would weave a mat in the day: but the old man used to take it and sell it, and spent the price of both mats in wine, and at nightfall would bring the brother home a paltry piece of bread. For three years he did thus, and the brother said no word. But at last the brother said to himself, "Here am I naked, and in want do I eat bread: I shall rise and go hence." But again he thought within himself and said, "Where am I to go? I shall stay here: for God's sake I shall stay in this common life." And thereupon appeared to him God's angel, and said, "Go not away, for tomorrow we shall come to thee." And the brother begged the old man that day, saying, "Go not away anywhere, for this day they come to take me." But the hour came when the old man was in the habit of going down to the town, and he said to the brother, "They will not come today, my son: for it is already late." And he said to him again and again that they would come: and even as he talked with him, he slept in peace. And the old man wept, saying, "Alas, my son, for the years that I have lived in heedlessness, and thou in thy brief time hast by patience saved thy soul." And from that day did he become a sober and reverend old man.

xix. They used to tell of a certain brother, how he was neighbour to a certain great old man, and that he used to go in and steal whatever the old man had in his cell. The old man saw him, but would not upbraid him, but forced himself to work the harder with his hands, saying, "I think that my brother is needy." And he exacted more from himself than was his wont and straitened his belly, so that in want did he eat bread.

Now when the old man came to die, the brethren stood about him. And gazing on him who thieved, he said to him, "Come close to me." And he held his hands and kissed them, saying, "I thank these hands, my brother, since because of them I go to the kingdom of God." And he, cut to the heart, did penance and became an upright monk, taking pattern from the deeds of that great old man.

BOOK XVII
Of Love

i. Said the abbot Antony: "I do not now fear God, but I love Him, for love casteth fear out of doors."

ii. Again he said, "That with our neighbour there is life and death: for if we do good to our brother, we shall do good to God: but if we scandalise our brother, we sin against Christ."

v. The abbot Marcus said to the abbot Arsenius, "Wherefore dost thou flee from us?" And the old man said, "God knows that I love you: but I cannot be with God and with men. A thousand and a thousand thousand of the angelic powers have one will: and men have many. Wherefore I cannot send God from me, and come and be with men."

vii. At one time the abbot John was climbing up from Scete with other brethren: and he who was by way of guiding them mistook the way: for it was night. And the brethren said to the abbot John, "What shall we do, Father, for the brother has missed the way, and we may lose ourselves and die?" And the old man said, "If we say aught to him, he will be cast down. But I shall make a show of being worn out and say that I cannot walk, but must lie here till morning." And he did so. And the others said, "Neither shall we go on, but shall sit down beside thee." And they sat down until morning, so as not to discountenance their brother.

xviii. A brother asked a certain old man, saying, "There be two brothers, and one of them is quiet in his cell, and prolongs his fast for six days, and lays much travail on himself: but the other tends the sick. Whose work is the more acceptable to God?" And the old man answered, "If that brother who carries his fast for six days were to hang himself up by the nostrils, he could not equal the other, who does service to the sick."

xix. A certain brother asked an old man saying, "Tell me, Father, wherefore is it that the monks travail in discipline and yet receive not such grace as the ancient Fathers had?" And the old man said to him, "Then was love so great that each man set his neighbour on high: but now hath love grown cold and the whole world is set in malice, and each doth pull down his neighbour to the lower room, and for this reason we come short of grace."

BOOK XVIII
Of Contemplation

i. A brother went to the cell of the abbot Arsenius in Scete, and looked through the window, and saw the old man as it were one flame: now, the brother was worthy to look upon such things. And after he had knocked, the old man came out, and saw the brother as one amazed, and said to him, "Hast thou been knocking here for long? Hast thou seen aught?" And he answered, "No." And he talked with him, and sent him away.

xii. The abbot Moses, who dwelt in Petra, was at one time sorely harried by lust: and when he could no longer endure to hold himself in his cell, he set out to tell it to the abbot Isidore: and the old man asked him to go back again to his cell. But he did not consent, saying, "I cannot, Father." And he took him and brought him into the house. And he said to him, "Look at the sunset." And he looked, and saw a multitude of demons: and they were in commotion, and rousing themselves to battle. And again the abbot Isidore said, "Look to the East." And he looked, and saw an innumerable multitude of angels in glory. Whereupon the abbot Isidore said, "Behold, these are they that are sent to aid: those that are climbing up in the west are they that fight against us: and they that are with us are more than they that be against us." And the abbot Moses thanked God and took courage, and returned to his cell.

[Here the translation by John the Subdeacon begins: in the *Vitae Patrum* it appears as a separate book.]

xxi.[20] At one time Zachary went to his abbot Silvanus, and found him in an ecstasy, and his hands were stretched out to heaven. And when he saw him thus, he closed the door and went away: and coming back about the sixth hour, and the ninth, he found him even so: but toward the tenth hour he knocked, and coming in found him lying quiet and said to him, "What ailed thee today, Father?" And he said, "I was ill today, my son." But the young man held his feet saying, "I shall not let thee go, until thou tell me what thou hast seen." The old man answered him: "I was caught up into heaven, and I saw the glory of God. And I stood there until now, and now am I sent away."

BOOK XX

Of the Excellent Way of Life
of Divers Holy Men[21]

i. The abbot Dulas told this tale: "At one time when Bessarion, my abbot, and I were walking in the desert, we came near a cave: and entering in, we found there a certain brother sitting and making a plait of palm-leaves: and he would not look upon us, nor give us greeting nor have any speech with us. So the old man said to me, 'Let us go hence, it may be that it is not in this brother's heart to speak with us.' And we went out from thence and straightway walked to see the abbot John. Coming back we passed again by the cave where we had seen that brother, and the old man said to me, 'Let us go in to visit that brother, if haply God hath put it in his heart to speak with us.' And entering in we found him, that he had slept in peace. But the old man said to me, 'Come, brother, let us lift up his body: for this one end hath God sent us, that we may bury him.' And when we were lifting him up, we found that it was a woman. And the old man marvelled, saying, 'Behold how women struggle against the devil in the desert, and we in the cities live in dishonour.' And glorifying God who hath a care for them that love him, we departed thence."

iv. The abbot Sisois was dwelling alone in the mountain of the abbot Antony: for his servant tarried in coming to him, and for ten months he saw no man. But as he walked upon the mountain, he found a certain Pharanite herding cattle. And the old man said to him, "Whence comest thou, and how long hast thou been here?" And he said, "Indeed, Father, I have had eleven months on this mountain, and I have not seen a man except thee." And the old man, hearing it, went into his cell and smote himself, saying, "Lo, Sisois, thou didst think thou hadst done somewhat, and thou hast not done as much as this man that is of the world."

v. This same abbot Sisois siting in his cell would ever have his door closed. But it was told of him how in the day of his sleeping, when the Fathers were sitting round him, his face shone like the sun, and he said to them, "Look, the abbot Antony comes." And after a little while, he said again to them, "Look, the company of the prophets comes." And again his face shone brighter, and he said, "Look, the company of the apostles comes." And his face shone with a double glory, and lo, he seemed as though he spoke with others. And the old man entreated him, saying, "With whom art thou speaking, Father?" And he said to them, "Behold, the angels came to take me, and I asked that I might be left a little while to repent." The old men said to him, "Thou has no need of repentance, Father." But he said to them "Verily I know not if I have clutched at the very beginning of repentance." And they all knew that he was made perfect. And again of a sudden his face was as the sun, and they all were in dread. And he said to them, "Look, behold the Lord cometh, saying, 'Bring me my chosen from the desert.'" And straightway he gave up the ghost. And there came as it might be lightning, and all the place was filled with sweetness.

xvi. They told of the same abbot Macarius the elder that he was once walking in the desert, and found the head of a dead man lying on the ground: and when he stirred it with the staff of palm that he had in his hand, the head spoke to him. The old man said to it, "Who art thou?" And that head answered the old man, "I was a priest of the heathen that used to dwell in this place, but thou art the abbot Macarius, who hast the Holy Spirit of God. Wherefore in whatever hour thou hast had pity on them that are in torment and hast prayed for them, then are they a little consoled." The old man said to him, "What is this consolation?" That head made answer, "As far as the sky is distant from the earth, so deep is the fire beneath our feet and above our head. And standing in the midst of the fire, there is not one of us can see his neighbour face to face. [But when thou dost pray for us, we look one upon the other, and this doth pass with us for consolation."]²² Then said the old man, weeping, "Woe to the day in which man was born, if this be the consolation of his pain."

BOOK XXI
Divers Sayings²³

xvi. A certain philosopher questioned the holy Antony. "How," said he, "dost thou content thyself, Father, who art denied the comfort of books?" He answered, "My book, philosopher, is the nature of created things, and as often as I have a mind to read the words of God, it is at my hand."

xvii. One came to the abbot Macarius, in the great heat of noon, burning with thirst, and asked for water to drink. "Let this shade," said he, "suffice thee, for many a wayfarer on land or on the sea is now in want of it, and hath no pleasure of it."

xxvi. A certain old man said, "If thou makest discourse to any of eternal life, speak to him that hears thee with compunction and with tears: speak not otherwise, lest thou be found empty, hasting to save others with alien speech. For God saith to the sinner, *What hast thou to do to declare My Righteousness, or take My covenant in thy mouth?* Say, therefore, 'I am a dog, nay a dog is better than I, in that he loveth his master, and shall not come to judgment.'"

xxx. An old man was asked by a certain soldier if God received a penitent man. And after heartening him with many words, he said to him at the last, "Tell me, beloved, if thy cloak were torn, wouldst throw it away?" He said, "Nay, but I would patch it and wear it." The old man said to him, "If thou wouldst spare thy garment, shall not God have mercy on His own image?"

THE SAYINGS OF
THE FATHERS

from the Greek by an unknown translator

This anonymous collection (Book III of the *Vitae Patrum*), has a good deal of material in common with Pelagius and Paschasius of Dumes, but it is curiously individual. Rosweyde assigned it boldly to Rufinus. He had not, he said, so sensitive a nose as St. Jerome's in tracking a style, but to his mind, whoever was responsible for the *Historia Monachorum* was responsible for this.[1] The argument from style is dangerous, for here it varies from a warm muffled prose to the plain austerity of Pelagius. Yet the more elaborate stories are very close to the longer-winded sections of the *Historia*:[2] there is the same evident pleasure in using two abstract nouns for one, and in multiplying relative causes, the same earnestness to edify, the same deep kindness. Now and then Pelagius and he tell the same story: and the advantage is not always with Pelagius. "God, Thou art no longer necessary to us, that Thou shouldst be anxious for us" *(Deus, iam non es nobis necessarius ut pro nobis sis sollicitus)* is only an exaggeration of Pelagius, "We have no longer need that Thou shouldst think of us" *(Deus, iam te opus non habemus cogitare de nobis),* but the reader is at once aware that the first translator felt the humour of the situation: he is not certain of the second. The same sense of comedy, and the same delight in a phrase, are in the story of the brethren who came out to the desert to be edified by its frugality and had more of it than they bargained for; Pelagius' version is only the skeleton. Again, in the story of how Macarius, carrying home his palm leaves, met the Evil One, the unknown translator adds the word *diluculo,* "at dawn," and gives the scene its quality of a Chinese sepia drawing. Again, when Serapion sold his single gospel and said, "I have but sold that word which ever said to me, *Sell that thou hast,"* it was the unknown who added the "ever," and made the voice living and haunting.[3] The Socratic story, told only here, of the old abbot Poemen hearing a brother commended because he hated evil, and asking, "What is it, to hate evil?" is enough in itself to justify the collection.[4] There is character in an anthology, and Rosweyde's unwarrantable ascription is obstinate in the mind. For the compiler was clumsy, sententious, shrewd and gentle: Grunnius, in short, walking his tortoise walk.

THE SAYINGS OF THE FATHERS

v. At one time certain brethren went forth from their monastery to visit the Fathers who dwelt in the desert. And on their coming to a certain aged hermit, he welcomed them with great joy and as the custom is, set a little meal before them. For he saw that they were tired after their journey, and so he made them eat before the ninth hour, and whatever he had in his cell he set down for them to eat, and made much of them. And when evening was come, they recited the customary prayers and psalms, and at night they did likewise. Now the old man was lying quiet by himself in a place apart, and he heard them talking among themselves and saying: "These hermits keep a better and more plentiful table than we who live in monasteries." And the old man heard it and held his peace. And when day broke, they took the road to visit another hermit, who lived in the neighbourhood of the old man. But as they were going out the old man said to them: "Greet him from me and say to him, 'Be careful not to water the vegetables.'" So when they came to the other old man, they gave him the message. And he understood the reason of it, and kept the brothers with him, and gave them baskets to weave, himself sitting with them, and working without a pause. When evening was come at the lighting of the lamps he added others to the wonted psalms, and when prayers were ended he said to them: "It is indeed not our custom to eat every day, but since you have come we must make a feast today": and he set dry bread before them, and salt, saying, "On your account we must make better cheer," and he set out a little vinegar and salt and a trifle of oil: and when they had risen from table, he again began upon the psalter till it was close on dawn: and he said to them: "Since you are here, we cannot sing the whole canon, because you must rest a little, being weary from your journey." When morning had come, they would fain have left him at Prime, but the old man would not suffer it, saying: "Rather must you order it to stay with us several days: I shall not let you go today, but for love's sake keep you another three." And when they heard that, they rose by night and they stole away from that place before the day would break.

xxiii. There were two brethren, monks, that lived together in a cell, whose humility and patience were the praise of many, even from among the Fathers. A certain saintly man, hearing of them, wished to prove if their humility was sincere and perfect: so he came to visit them. They welcomed him joyfully and when the wonted prayers and psalms were ended, he went out of doors and saw a little garden where they grew their vegetables. And he caught up a stick, and set to with all his might to beat and break down the herbs, till not one was left. The brothers saw him but said not a word, nor were their faces vexed or downcast. He came again into the cell, and when Vespers was said, they bowed before him, saying: "If you will suffer it, master, we shall go and cook and eat the cabbage that is left, because this is the time that we have our meal." Then the old man bowed before them, saying: "I thank my God, for that I see the Holy Ghost rest upon you: and I exhort and entreat you, brothers beloved, that ye keep to the end this virtue of holy humility and patience, for it shall be your greatness and glory in heaven in the sight of God."

xxiv. There was in a monastery a certain old man, of most reverend life, and he fell into grievous sickness: and he was wasted with great and intolerable weakness and for a long time travailed in distress, nor could the brethren find any way to succour him, for those things which his sickness required they had not in the monastery. But a certain handmaid of God, hearing of his affliction, entreated the abbot of the monastery that she might take him to her own cell and tend him, more especially as she could more easily find in the city such things as were needful to his sickness. So the abbot of the monastery commanded the brethren to carry him to the cell of the handmaid of God. And she received the old man with all reverence, and for God's sake tended him, in hope of that eternal recompense, which she trusted to receive from our Saviour Christ. For three years and more she had watchfully tended the servant of God, when men of evil heart began to suspect according to the itching of their own minds that the old man was not clean in his conscience towards the virgin that tended him. And the old man hearing it, entreated the divinity of Christ, saying, "Thou, Lord our God, who alone knowest all things and seest the griefs of my sickness and my misery, and dost consider this infirmity which for so long had wasted me, so that I had need of the nursing of this handmaid of thine, who hath tended me for Thy sake: give unto her, my Lord, her great and due reward in the life eternal, even as Thou didst promise in Thy mercy to such as showed kindness for Thy sake to the poor and the sick." And when the day of his passing had drawn nigh, many of the older brethren of the monastery, holy men, came about him, and the old man said to them: "I beseech you, my lords and fathers, and brethren, that when I am dead ye take my staff, and plant it on my grave, and if it take root and come to fruit, then shall ye know that my conscience is clean towards this handmaid of God that tended me. But if it does not put forth leaves, know that I am not clean of her." When therefore the man of God had gone out of the body, the holy fathers planted his staff upon the grave, as he had bidden, and it brought forth leaves, and when the time had come, it bore fruit: and they all marvelled and glorified God. Many came from the neighbouring parts at such a miracle, and magnified the grace of the Saviour, and we ourselves saw the little tree: and we blessed God who in all things defendeth them that serve him in sincerity and truth.

xxvi. The holy old men told us this story, how there was a certain monk in the desert of Scete: and he came to visit the holy Fathers in the place which is called Cellia, where a multitude of monks dwell in separate cells. And since he could not at the time find a cell to live in, one of the old men who had another cell empty gave it to him, saying, "Meantime, rest in this cell, until thou findest one wherein to abide." Now a great number of the brethren began to come to visit him, desiring to hear from him some word of the life eternal: for he had the spiritual grace of teaching the word of God. And the old man who had offered him the cell saw it, and his heart was wounded with envy and spite, and he began to wax indignant and to say, "For so long time have I dwelt in this place and the brethren come not to me save very rarely, and that on feast days, and lo well nigh every day do the brethren go in crowds to this impostor": and he said to his disciple, "Go and tell him to go out from that cell, because I have need of it." But when his disciple came to that brother, he said to him, "My abbot hath sent me to thy holiness, to pray thee to send him word by me how thou dost: for he hath heard that thou art sick." And the brother sent back word by him, "Pray for me, my lord and father, for indeed I have sore pain in my stomach." So the disciple came back and said to his abbot, "He entreats thy holiness that thou will grant him two days grace to provide himself with another cell." Three days passed, and again he sent his disciple, saying, "Go, bid him go out from my cell, for if he again puts it off, tell him that I will straightway come and beat him out of my cell with my staff." So the disciple made his way to the aforesaid brother, and said, "My abbot is sorely distressed for thine infirmity, and hath sent me to ask if thou art better." And he answered and said, "I give thanks, my good lord, to thy loving kindness, that thou dost take anxious thought for me, but verily am I recovered by thy prayers." The disciple returning said to his abbot, "Lo, now he prays thy holiness to wait until the Sunday, and then he will straightway go out." But when Sunday came, and he had not gone, the old man took his stick, flaming with spite and wrath, and set forth to turn him out of his cell with blows. But his disciple coming to join him said, "If it please thee, Father, I shall go before thee and see lest perchance some of the brethren be come to greet him, and if they should see thee, they might be scandalised." So the disciple went ahead and going in said to him, "Behold, my abbot cometh to greet thee, so go swiftly out and meet him by way of gratitude, since his great love and kindness for thee hath brought him to visit thee." And he straightway rose up and ran to meet him with all eagerness. And when he saw him, before they had come close, he fell on his face on the ground, and did reverence to the old man with all gratitude, saying, "May God reunite thee, Father most dear, with good everlasting for this thy cell, which thou didst offer me for His name's sake, and may the Lord Christ prepare thee a mansion glorious and splendid in the heavenly Jerusalem among His saints."

Hearing this, the old man was pricked to the heart, and throwing away his stick he ran into his arms, and kissed him and invited him to his own cell, and together they gave thanks and did eat. But the old man called his disciple and questioned him saying, "Tell me, my son, if thou didst say to this brother the words about the cell that I commissioned thee to say to him?" Then his disciple confessed to him, saying, "In truth, my lord, I tell thee that because of the humility which I owe to thee as my father and lord, I did not dare to answer thee aught when thou didst send me to him: nevertheless I told him none of the things that thou didst command me." And hearing this, the old man straightway fell at his feet saying, "From this day forth thou art my father, and I thy disciple: for by thy hasting and tarrying and all thy doing in the fear and loving kindness of God, the Lord Christ hath set free my soul and my brother's from the snare of sin." For in faith and holy anxiety and watchfulness did this disciple perfectly love his abbot in the charity of Christ, and was in sore dread lest through envy and wrath his spiritual father should so act as to lose all those holy labours which he had wrought in serving Christ from his youth, for the rewards of the life everlasting. And the Lord gave them His grace, that they rejoiced in Christ's peace together.

xlvi. The abbot Silvanus with Zachary his disciple, came to a certain monastery, and before they took their leave, the monks made them eat a little. But after they had gone out, his disciple came on water, and would fain have drunk. Then said Silvanus,

"Zachary, today is a fast." He said, "But, Father, did we not eat today?" The old man said, "That was love's bread, my son: but for us, let us keep our own fast."

xlviii. One of the fathers used to say, "One man is found eating much and yet refraining while he is still hungry, lest he be filled: and another eats little, and is filled. He who eats much and refrains while he is still hungry, hath more merit than he who eats little and is full fed."

li. One of the Fathers fell ill, and for many days could touch no food. But one of his disciples urged him, saying, "If you will let me, my father, I shall make you a little cake." And the old man nodded, and he made it. Now beside him was a little pot of honey, and another similar pot with linseed oil, and it was stinking and good for nothing, unless perchance for a lamp: and the brother by mistake put some of it in the cake, thinking that he was putting in honey. The old man tasted it, and said nothing, but ate in silence: but when it was given him a third time, he said: "I cannot eat, my son." But the young man, coaxing him, said, "Look, Father, they are good cakes and I am eating some myself," and then when he had tasted it, and knew what he had done, he fell on his face saying, "Woe is me, Father, for I have killed thee: thou hast laid this sin upon me, because thou didst say no word." And the old man said, "Vex not thyself, my son, because of it: for if God had willed that I should eat a good cake, thou wouldst have put in the honey, and not this that thou didst put in."

liv. There was a gathering in the church on a feast day, and while the other monks were eating, one of them said to those serving, "As I eat nothing that has been cooked, I bid thee bring me salt." At this, the brother serving shouted to another, in the hearing of all, "Since this brother eats no cooked meats, bring him a little salt." Then said the blessed Theodore, "It had profited thee more, my brother, to eat flesh in thy cell, than to hear this spoken in the presence of the brethren."

lv. A stranger monk came to the abbot Silvanus in Mount Sinai, and saw the brethren busy in the fields and said to them, "Wherefore do ye labour for the meat that perisheth? For Mary chose that good part." Then said the old man to Zachary his disciple, "Give him a codex to read, and put him in a cell that has nothing in it." By the ninth hour, however, the brother was gazing up and down the road, to see if perchance the old man would call him to a meal. And when the hour had gone by, he came to the old man, and said, "Are the brethren not eating today, Father?" And when the old man said they were, "Wherefore," said he, "didst thou not call me?" Then said the abbot Silvanus, "Thou art a spiritual man, and thou dost not hold food to be necessary: but we being carnal have need to eat, and to that end we work: but thou hast chosen that good part. For thou readest all day and hast no wish for carnal food." And on hearing this, he began to be ashamed and said, "Forgive me, Father." And the abbot Silvanus answered him, "So Martha is necessary to Mary, for because of Martha is Mary praised."

lxi. While the abbot Macarius was living in that part of the desert where he alone had his dwelling (for the lower desert was full of brethren), he was looking down the road one evening, and saw the Devil come in the shape of a man, wearing a linen tunic full of holes, and from every hole a little jar was dangling: and the old man said to him, "Whither away, Malignant?" And he made answer, "I go to stir up these brethren that are down below." And the old man said, "And why take so many little jars with thee?" And he said, "I bring some relish for the brethren, and the reason why I carry so many is that if one is not to their liking, I show another, and if that does not please, I hold out another: and it cannot be but that some one of them all will serve."

And so saying he departed. But the old man remained there looking down the road until he should return, and when he was coming back, he said to him, "May it be well with thee." But the Devil said, "How canst thou say that, when they have all turned contrary to me, and not one of them will heed my advice?" And the old man said, "So thou hast no friend at all?" But the Devil said, "One friend I have, that agrees with me, and whenever he sees me, he will turn this way or that, as simple as you please." And when he was asked the name, he said, "He is called Theopemptus." He took his departure, and with that the abbot Macarius rose up and went down to the lower desert. And when the brethren heard it, they came out to meet him, and each made preparation, hoping that Macarius would abide in his cell. But he asked for the cell of Theopemptus and made his way thither. And when he had been joyfully received and they were sitting together by themselves, the old man said to him, "How is it with thee, my son?" And he answered, "Thanks to thy prayers, I am well." And the old man said, "Do thoughts not trouble thee?" And he answered, "For the time being I am well." For he was ashamed to say it. And the old man said to him, "Look you, after so many years in the desert, and held in honour by all, and at my age, for I am an old man, my thoughts torment me." And Theopemptus made answer, "Believe me, Father, they do the like with me." Then the old man invented one by one the imaginations that as it might be harried him, until Theopemptus had confessed it all. Then he said to him, "How dost thou fast?" He said, "Until the ninth hour." And the old man said, "Fast until evening, and meditate always without ceasing on somewhat from the Gospel or the other Scriptures; and as often as any unclean thought comes upon thee, never look down, but up, and God shall be swift to help." And soon thereafter the abbot Macarius departed into his own solitude. And again looking down the road, he saw the Devil returning, and asked him, "Whither away?" And he answered, "To stir up the brethren as before." But when he was coming back, he asked him how the brethren did. And he answered, "Ill, for they are all become rustic, and, what is more than all, he that I had for a friend and that did what I bade him, has turned round, I know not how, and seemed to me harsher by far than any of them." And he swore that he would not go there again, not in a great while: and so saying, he departed.

lxx. A certain monk Serapion owned a Gospel: and he sold it and gave to the hungry, following the memorable saying: for, said he, "I sold that same word that ever used to say to me 'Sell that thou hast and give to the poor.'"

lxxii. The abbot Paul used to say, "If a monk will have aught in his cell beyond those things without which he cannot live, he is often forced to go out from his cell, and is waylaid by the Demon." And Paul himself, through a whole Lent, lived on a pint of lentils and one small vessel of water, and busied himself on a single mat, plaiting and replaiting, that he might not have to go out of doors.

lxxiii. When the abbot Macarius was in Egypt, he had gone out of his cell: and returning found someone stealing whatever he had in his cell. So he stood by as if himself had been a stranger, and helped load the animal with all stealth and led him out, saying, "We brought nothing into the world. The Lord gave, and the Lord hath taken away: and as He willed, so is it come to pass. Blessed be the Lord in all things."

lxxvii. One of the brethren, that had been insulted by another, came to the abbot Sisois and told him the scorn that had been put upon him, and said, "I am set to revenge myself, Father." And the old man began to entreat him to leave vengeance to God. But he said, "I shall not stay till I have stoutly avenged myself." So the old man said, "Since thou hast made up thy mind once for all, now let us pray," and rising, he began to pray in these words, "God, Thou art no longer necessary to us, that Thou needst be anxious for us: for we ourselves, as this brother hath said, are both willing and able to avenge ourselves." But when the brother heard it, he fell at the old man's feet seeking his pardon, and promised that he would contend no more with the man against whom he was angered.

xciii. There was a certain old man in Egypt, and before the abbot Poemen came to that place, he was held in great worship by all. But when the abbot Poemen came down thither from Scete, many abandoned the old man and came to him, and because of this the old man began to envy him and carp at him. And hearing of it, the abbot Poemen was saddened and said to his brethren, "What shall we do? These men have brought trouble upon us, for they have deserted so holy an old man, and look to us that are naught. How shall we heal this great man of his hurt? Come, let us make ready a little food and make our way to him carrying it, and a little wine, and sup with him, and perchance in this way we might soothe his soul." So they set out and knocked at his door. But the old man's disciple, hearing them, said, "Who be ye?" And they answered, "Tell thy abbot that Poemen hath come to seek a blessing from him." But when the old man heard it from this disciple, he answered him, "Go and say to them, 'Go your ways, for I am not at leisure.'" Nevertheless they stayed there sorrowful, saying, "We shall not go from hence, till we have been found worthy to kneel before him." And when he saw their humility and their patience, he was sorry and opened the door and they kissed one another and did sup together. And the old man said to him, "In truth it is not only the works that I have heard of thee, but I have seen in thee a hundredfold more." And from that day he was made his dearest friend.

xcvi. There were two old men living together in one cell, and never had there risen even the paltriest contention between them. So the one said to the other, "Let us have one quarrel the way other men do." But the other said, "I do not know how one makes a quarrel." The first said, "Look, I set a tile between us and say, 'That is mine,' and do thou say, 'It is not thine, it is mine.' And thence arises contention and squabble." So they set the tile between them, and the first one said, "That is mine," and the second made reply: "I hope that it is mine." And the first said, "It is not thine: it is mine." To which the second made answer, "If it is thine, take it." After which they could find no way of quarrelling.

c. A certain brother asked the abbot Poemen, saying, "What am I to do, Father, for I am troubled by sadness?" The old man said to him, "Look to no man for aught, condemn no man, disparage no man: and God shall give thee rest."

cxxiv. When the abbot Macarius, carrying palm leaves, was returning to his cell at dawn, the Devil met him with a keen-edged sickle, and would have struck him and could not. And crying out at him "Great," he said, "is the violence I suffer from thee, O Macarius, that when I fain would injure thee, I cannot: yet whatever thou dost, I do also, and more. For thou dost fast now and then, but by no food am I ever refreshed. Thou dost often keep vigil; no slumber ever falls upon me. But in one thing thou dost overmaster me, I do myself confess it." And when the blessed Macarius asked him what that might be, "It is thy humility alone," he said, "that masters me." He spoke, and the blessed Macarius stretched out his hands in prayer: and the evil spirit vanished into the air.

cxxvi. One of the Fathers used to say, "Every labour of the monk, without humility, is vain. For humility is the forerunner of love, as John was the forerunner of Jesus, drawing all men to him: even so humility draws to love, that is to God Himself, for God is love."

cxxvii. Once when the abbot Macarius was climbing up the mountain in Nitria, he bade his disciple go a little way before him. And as he went on ahead, he met a priest of the idols, hurrying swiftly, and carrying a great log. And the disciple shouted at him, "Whither so fast, devil?" At which the irate priest beat him so soundly that he left him half dead: and again hurried on his way. A little further on, he met the blessed Macarius, who said to him, "May it be well with thee, O toiler, may it be well!" The priest, in surprise, said "What good dost thou see in me that thou shouldst wish me well?" To which the old man made answer, "Because I see thee toiling and hasting, thou knowest not why." And the priest said, "And I, moved by thy salutation, knew thee for a great servant of God: now some other miserable monk, I know not who, met me and threw insults at me, but I gave him back blows for words." Then, seizing the feet of the blessed Macarius, he cried to him, "Unless thou makest me a monk, I shall not let thee go." So taking the road together they came to the place where the stricken brother lay, whom they both lifted up, and as he could not walk, they carried him in their arms to the church. But when the brethren saw the priest in company with the blessed Macarius they were dumbfounded: and in wonderment they made him a monk, and because of him many pagans were made Christian. And the abbot Macarius would say, "That a proud and ill speech would turn good men to evil, but a good and humble speech would turn evil men to better."

cxxxii. Certain brothers were sitting near the abbot Poemen; and one brother began praising another, saying "That brother is a good man, for he hates evil." The old man spoke and said, "And what is it, to hate evil?" He knew not how to answer: and himself asked, saying, "Tell me, Father, what is it to hate evil?" And the old man said, "He hates evil, who hates his own sins, and who blesseth and loveth every one of his brethren."

cxxxvii. The abbot Isaac came once into the monastery and saw there a careless brother and in anger commanded that he be expelled from the monastery. And when he had gone out and was nearing his own house, there came God's angel and stood before the door of his cell, saying, "I shall not suffer thee to enter." Then he asked that he might be shown his fault. And the angel made answer and said, "God sent me, saying, 'Go, and say to Isaac, Where dost thou command Us to send this brother who hath sinned?'" Then did he straightway repent, saying, "Lord, I have sinned, have mercy upon me." And the angel said, "Arise, the Lord will have mercy. But do not the like again, to condemn any, before God hath judged him."

cxxxviii. It chanced that a certain brother in a monastery fell into disgrace: and whilst the others were upbraiding him, he made his way to the abbot Antony. And the brethren followed him, wishful to bring him back, and began to cover him with reproaches, he meantime denying that he had committed that fault. Now the abbot Paphnutius was there, whose surname was Cephalus, and he told the brethren in assembly a parable that they had never heard. "I saw," said he, "on the bank of the river a man sunk to his knees in the mud; and some came up with outstretched hands to pull him out, and sank him up to the neck." Then said the blessed Antony of the blessed Paphnutius, "Behold a man who can verily heal the soul." And the brethren cut to the heart by his discourse did penance and restored to the community the brother who had gone from it.

cxxxix. One of the old men said, "If thou shalt see any man sinning, cast not the blame on him, but on him that fighteth with him, saying, 'Woe is me, for here is this man conquered against his will, even as I: and do thou weep and seek the comforting of God, for we all are deceived.'"

cxl. A certain Timothy, a hermit, heard of a certain heedless brother: and when his abbot asked him what should be done with him, gave his counsel to cast him out from the monastery. Now after he had been cast out, temptation came to Timothy: and when he was confessing in the presence of God and saying, "Have mercy upon me," there came to him a voice saying, "Timothy, this tribulation came to thee for this one thing, that thou hast despised thy brother in the time of his temptation."

cxlii. An old man said, "If any enjoin somewhat upon his brother in the fear of God and in humility, that word which was spoken for God's sake compels the brother to obey, and to do what was enjoined upon him. But if any anxious to rule hath chosen to command his brother not according to the fear of God but for the sake of his own authority and his own will, He who seeth the secrets of the heart will not suffer him to hear, lest he should do what was commanded him; for that which is done for God's sake is manifestly a work of God: and that which was ordained for pride's sake is manifestly the authority of men. Whatsoever things are from God, have their spring in humbleness: but such things as spring from authority and anger and strife, these are of the Enemy."

cxlvii. Another old man had finished his baskets and was putting handles on them, when he heard his neighbour saying, "What shall I do, for the fair day is near, and I have nothing to make handles for my baskets?" And the old man unfastened his own handles and brought them to his brother, saying, "Look, I have these to spare, take and put them on thy baskets," and so for the great love that he had he saw to it that his brother's work was rightly finished, and left his own imperfect.

clvi. The abbot Agatho, coming into the city to sell his work, found a stranger lying in an alley sick, and with none to care for him: and the old man stayed there and hired a cell for himself, and tended the sick man and supported him with the work of his own hands. For four months he stayed there, till he had healed the sick man: and so returned again to his own cell.

THE SAYINGS OF
THE FATHERS

translated from the Greek by Paschasius the Deacon
for the Abbot Martin of Dumes

On March 20th, in the year 580, St. Martin, abbot of Dumes and archbishop of Braga, died. Gregory of Tours noted it in his chronicle, and added a brief biography of a man he had greatly admired, "so steeped in letters that he was second to no man of his time."[1] He was born in Pannonia, the fragment of Austria and Hungary that is bounded by the Danube flowing west through Vienna and south through Budapest. Like Jerome, who came from a county town just below its southern march, he went as a young man on a pilgrimage to the East, and came from it a missionary, to preach to a people still half-pagan in the northwestern corner of Spain. There he founded the abbey of Dumes, and in 572 was signing conciliar documents as Archbishop of Braga. Fortunatus wrote him a letter and poem of turgid compliment, full of reference to Cicero and Vergil; and St. Radegunde sent him messages of devotion.[2] That he had some knowledge of Greek is evident from his having worked upon the canons of the Eastern church, collating them with the original text;[3] and while still plain abbot and priest of Dumes and not yet archbishop, he gave his reluctant deacon Paschasius a Greek codex to be translated into Latin. The translation (now Book VII of the *Vitae Patrum*) was duly made; but it came accompanied with a prefatory letter that has no match among epistles dedicatory till one comes to Ben Jonson. There is no other source of information about Paschasius beyond these dozen lines: but in these he has contrived to fix his image, and the image of his type, vain and crabbed and obstinate, but an honest scholar.

"To his revered Father and Lord, Martin, abbot and priest, Paschasius.

"When you commanded me, my Father, to translate into Latin the *Vitae Patrum,* written with the usual studied elegance of the Greeks, I would, if I could, have balked at the unaccustomed task. For nothing can ever be written or read or fashioned on the anvil that runs counter to the temper and conviction of the heart. To say that I know I know nothing I dare not, lest I seem to filch the phrase from the wise Socrates. But since your command must no less be obeyed, I shall not vaunt myself in display of parts, but prove the loyalty I owe you in the task assigned. There are many Latin versions of the works of these well-spoken men, with which I know you familiar; if therefore you light on something from these books less elegantly phrased in mine, do not, I beg of you, throw the blame on me. Such things as I found written in the codex given me, and as they were written, so did I translate; though I cannot claim that the setting forth of them is absolute. . . . You commanded from me the writing; I entreat from you the polishing. For I shall have no confidence that anything here has pleased you, if I am told that nothing has displeased you."

It is an agreeable conjecture, though only a conjecture, that the codex over which Paschasius grumbled had been brought by St. Martin from his travels in the East. That he brought at any rate the spirit of the Desert with him is evident from the titles of the books that he wrote himself: on the outcasting of Boasting;

on the outcasting of Pride; on Humbleness; on the Habit and Effects of Anger, and how it may be softened (*leniatur*).[4] In addition to these, there is a collection, *Ægyptiorum Patrum Sententiae,* ascribed to him as translator in a Toledo manuscript, and found with the same ascription in a ninth-century manuscript of the abbey of St. Florian. It may have been a personal anthology made from various collections: it is a small one, of little over a hundred sayings, but quintessential, if indeed the quintessence of the Desert teaching is that a man should love mercy and walk humbly with men and God; and it ends with a memory, found only in this collection, of Macarius who shielded the brethren like an earthly God, and the injunction from the abbot Moses to look on one's own sins and not on one's neighbour's, and to keep a humble and a contrite heart. The manuscript ends with an ironic echo to that quiet benediction. "This book," writes the anonymous scribe by way of colophon, "was begun in Hunia (Hungary) with the army in the year of Our Lord 819, on the 2nd of June, and finished at St. Florian on the 12th of September, in the fifteenth week."[5] It was during a campaign of Louis the Pious, four years after Charlemagne's death; and in that fifteen weeks this unknown hand transcribed the lives of Antony, Paul, Hilarion, and Malchus; the *Historia Monachorum* translated by Rufinus; the first fifteen books of the *Verba Seniorum,* translated by Pelagius; the translation of Paschasius; and the small collection ascribed to Martin of Dumes. "The script was so ancient," said Aventinus, with the condescension of the sixteenth-century scholar, "that I had to become a boy again and go back to the elements." By the same condition, one enters the Kingdom of God.

THE SAYINGS OF THE FATHERS
I. Translated from the Greek by Paschasius

xxxv. 2. The blessed Antony was wont to say, "The Fathers of old went forth into the desert, and when themselves were made whole, they became physicians, and returning again they made others whole; but if it should come to pass that any of us go into the desert, we offer a cure to other men before we be cured ourselves: and our infirmity returns upon us and our last sins are worse than our first: for which cause is it commanded us 'Physician, look first to thyself.'"

xvii. 1. A certain brother asked the abbot Pimenion saying, "What is faith?" And the old man said, "To live ever in loving kindness and in humbleness, and to do good to one's neighbour."

v. 1. A certain brother asked an old man saying, "If a brother owes me a few pence, wouldst thou have me ask them of him?" And the old man said, "Speak to him of it but once, and in humility." But he said, "If I speak once, and he gives me naught, what am I to do?" Then the old man said, "Say naught to him more." But he said, "And what am I to do, for I cannot master my thoughts that would have me harry him?" And the old man said, "Put these thoughts out of thy mind and forbear to vex thy brother, for thou art a monk."

v. 2. At one time, when the abbot Silvanus had left his cell for a little while, his disciple Zachary and other brethren moved the fence of his garden and made the garden bigger. But when the old man came back and saw it, he took up his sheepskin to go away. And they cast themselves at his feet and asked him to tell them why he did thus. And the old man spoke, "I shall not go into this cell," he said, "until the fence be brought back into its place." Which being speedily done, he returned.

xii. 6. The abbot Sisois, sitting with another brother, was carried into an ecstasy, and unaware that the other was in hearing, sighed: and thereafter he began to reproach himself and say, "Brother, forgive me, I pray thee: I do now perceive that I am not yet a monk, in that I sighed in the hearing of another." For as often as the old man would stand to pray, and lifted his hands to heaven, swiftly would he bring them down again, so that if another were by, he would not reckon it to him for praise.

xviii. 2. A certain brother coming into Scete asked that he might see the abbot Arsenius. And when the other brethren would have persuaded him to rest a little, he made answer, "I shall not eat bread, until I come at a sight of him." Then one of the brethren led him to the cell of the abbot Arsenius, and knocking at his door, brought him in. And they were received, and prayer made, and they sat down. Now since the blessed Arsenius held his peace, he who had brought the brother said, "I take my leave." But the brother who had come out of a great desire, seeing that the abbot Arsenius had naught to say to him, was sitting silent and confused: and he said, "I, too, brother, will take my leave with thee." And so they both departed. Now he had also asked that he might be taken to the abbot Moses, him that had been converted from among thieves. And the abbot Moses received him, and kindly entertained him, and sent him away. Then the brother who had taken him to both said to him, "Behold, thou hast seen both those whom thou didst desire to see: which of the two is more to thy liking?" And he said, "To my mind, he seems to me the better who gave us good welcome and a good meal." And one of the Fathers heard what he had said, and prayed to the Lord saying, "Lord, reveal to me this, I pray Thee, how one man for Thy sake withdraws himself from all sight and speech of men, and another for Thy sake is a good fellow with all." And behold, in a trance, he was shown two

ships upon the river: in one he saw the Holy Ghost sailing together with the abbot Arsenius in silence and in peace: and in
the other ship he saw the abbot Moses and the angels of God,
and they were giving him honey and the honeycomb into his
mouth.

2. *Ascribed to Martin, Abbot of Dumes*

i. The abbot John used to say to his disciples, "The Fathers did
eat only bread and salt and were made strong in the work of
God, whilst they straitened themselves: wherefore let us confine
ourselves to this same bread and salt. For it behoves them that
serve God to be straitened in themselves, for the Lord Himself
said, *Strait is the gate and narrow is the way that leadeth unto life.*"

ii. A brother asked the same old man saying, "These fasts and
vigils that we keep, what do they do?" He answered, "They
bring it about that the soul becomes humble. For it is written,
Look upon my humility and my pain, and forgive all my sins. For if
the soul travaileth in these, God will have compassion, and suffer with it."

iii. The abbot Poemen said, "With the imagination of lust and
the disparaging of thy neighbour, with these two speak not in
thy heart, nor consent to any of their befouling in thy soul. For
if thou hast suffered thy heart to dwell on these, thou shalt soon
feel their poisoning: it is the stirring of perdition: but by prayer
and good actions bring the malignant spirit to naught, and do
thou fight them off more hardily, and thou shalt have quiet."

iv. A brother asked an old man saying, "What shall I do, Fa-
ther, against thoughts of passion?" He answered, "Pray to the
Lord that the eyes of thy soul may behold the help that is from
God, that doth go round about a man and keep him safe."

v. A certain brother going to market questioned the abbot

Poemen and said, "How am I to sell my work?" And the old man said to him, "Seek not to sell it for more than it is worth, but rather if thou art vexed, be friend to him that would beat thee down, and sell it in peace. For when I myself have gone now and then to the market, I have never desired to please myself in the price of my work, and vex my brother, having this hope that my brother's gain will bring forth fruit."

xvii. The brethren asked the abbot Poemen concerning a certain brother that did fast for six days out of the seven with perfect abstinence, but was extreme choleric, and for what reason did he suffer it? And the old man made answer, "He that hath taught himself to fast for six days and not to control his temper, it would become him better to bring greater zeal to a lesser toil."

xviii. The abbot Poemen had a monk, a near kinsman, with him in the cell: and he had a controversy with another brother that lived outside the monastery: and the abbot Poemen said to him, "Brother kinsman, I like it not that thou shouldst have words with anyone outside our monastery." But he would not heed him. So the abbot Poemen rose up and came to another great old man and said to him, "My kinsman brother hath a controversy with a certain one outside our monastery, and we have no peace." And the old man said to him, "What, Poemen, art thou yet alive? Go to thy cell and lay it to thy heart that thou hast been a year in thy grave."

xix. At one time the abbot Poemen was sitting in his cell, and the brethren fell out mightily among themselves, and the old man spake to them no word at all. But the abbot Paphnutius came in and found them squabbling and said to him, "Wherefore hast thou left these brethren alone and hast not spoken to them that they should not quarrel?" And Poemen said to him, "They be brethren, they will make it up again." Paphnutius said to him, "What? Thou seest that in their squabble they have come nigh to bloodshed, and thou sayest that they will make it up again?" And Poemen said to him, "Brother, lay it to thy heart that I am not here." So quiet and silent, in all charity, was the abbot Poemen.

xx. At one time there came heretics to the abbot Poemen, and they began to speak ill of the archbishop of Alexandria: but the old man kept silence. But calling his disciple he said to him, "Set the table, and give them to eat, and so send them away in peace."

xxii. A brother asked an old man saying, "My heart is hard, and doth not fear God: what shall I do, that I may fear God?" He made answer, "I think myself that if a man would for ever accuse himself in his heart, he would come to the fear of God." The brother said, "What is it, to accuse one's self?" The old man answered, "That in every conjecture he should accuse his soul, saying to it that he must stand before God, and again should say, *Why should I bear any malice against man?* For I think that if a man would abide in these things the fear of God would come upon his soul."

xxiii. The abbot Macarius said, "If to a monk scorn hath become as praise, and poverty as riches, and hunger as feasting, he shall never die. For it is not possible that a man who doth rightly believe and doth loyally worship God, should fall into uncleanly passion and the error of the demons."

xxiv. An old man said, "Rising and walking and sitting, if God is before thine eyes, there is naught in which the Enemy can affright thee. If that thought abides in a man, the strength of God shall cleave to him."

xlix. The abbot Moses came to the well to draw water, and he saw the brother Zachary praying, and the Spirit of God resting over him.

lxx. The abbot Poemen said with a groan, "All virtues are gone into my cell but one, and by it doth a man stand." And the brethren asked him what that great virtue might be. And the old man said, "That a man should ever be rebuking himself."

lxxxiii. An old man said, "See that thou despise not the brother that stands by thee: for thou knowest not whether the spirit of God be in thee or in him."

xci. An old man said, "There is no stronger virtue than to scorn no man."

xciv. An old man said, "The man that every hour hath death before his eyes, will conquer meanness of soul."

xcv. An old man said, "Be a free man in thy speech, not a slave."

xcviii. An old man said, "In whatever place thou sittest, look not to them that have their consolation, but to the poor that have nor bread nor rest."

cvii. They said of the abbot Macarius the elder, that even as God doth protect all the world, and beareth the sins of men, so was he to the brethren as it might be an earthly God, for he covered up their faults, and what things he saw or heard, it was as though he saw not and heard not.

cix. These be seven sayings which the abbot Moses spake to the abbot Poemen, which, if any keep, whether he be set in a monastery or in solitude, or in the world itself, he can be saved.

1. First, as it is written, a man should love God with all his soul and all his understanding.

2. A man should love his neighbour as himself.

3. A man should mortify himself from all evil.

4. A man ought not to judge his brother in any conjuncture.

5. A man ought to do no hurt to any.

6. A man ought, before he go out from the body, to cleanse himself from all foulness of the flesh and spirit.

7. A man ought always to have a contrite and a humble heart. And this can he accomplish, who looks ever on his own sins and not on his neighbour's, by the succouring grace of our Lord Jesus Christ, who with God the Father and the Holy Ghost liveth and reigneth world without end. Amen.

OF ACCIDIE:
OF MORTIFICATION

by Cassian of Marseilles

The *Verba Seniorum* have something of the direct quick speech of the Synoptic Gospels; Cassian's *Collationes,* the brooding quiet of the Gospel according to St. John. He had had his youth in a monastery at Bethlehem;[1] a young man's hunger for the absolute sent him on pilgrimage to the Egyptian desert, to the Thebaid, and to Scete, which was already becoming a legend. There he spent the last decade of the fourth century. Late middle age found him abbot of a religious house of his own founding in Marseilles, and appealed to by the bishop of Apt, in Vaucluse, to write down his memories, "the simple life of the saints in simple speech," for the brethren of a new "rude" monastery he himself had lately founded.[2] Cassian hesitated: there was his own unworthiness to handle "things so hard, so secret, so holy," *res tam arduas, tam obscuras, tam sanctas;* there was the passage of so many years since he had shared that life: the knowledge that can be recaptured by no leisured meditation and no skill of words, but stands in experience alone.[3] Nevertheless he set down his memories: first in his *Foundations* and then in his *Conversations.* It is not the naked authentic speech of the Desert; time has dulled its edge, and the twenty years brooding of a sensitive mystic wraps the gaunt familiar figures round; it is as though they had entered into the cloud. But as Cassian

said of the monastic rule in France, one must temper the stern-
ness of Egypt because of the colder northern air, and bear in
mind the difficulty and diversity of men's lives. If proportion be
kept, there is equal perfection of observance, however unequal
the power;[4] the doctrine, in short, of relativity.

The two passages translated are not from his high rare moments of exaltation—their habitation is eternity. These illustrate
his ironic human perception, and make intelligible the more
alien experience of the desert, its concentration within the four
walls of one's cell. To read Cassian on Accidie is to recognise
the "white melancholy" of Gray in Pembroke, and the sullen
lethargy that is the sterile curse of the scholar and the artist. The
passage on mortification was spoken by the abbot Abraham,
in answer to Cassian's confession that he was sick for home, for
his own people and the house of his fathers, with its secret
woods and the richness of its fields, and all that gay and gentle
countryside.[5]

OF ACCIDIE: OF MORTIFICATION
1. Of Accidie

Our sixth contending is with that which the Greeks call
ακηδία, and which we may describe as tedium or perturbation
of heart. It is akin to dejection and especially felt by wandering
monks and solitaries, a persistent and obnoxious enemy to such
as dwell in the desert, disturbing the monk especially about
midday, like a fever mounting at a regular time, and bringing its
highest tide of inflammation at definite accustomed hours to the
sick soul. And so some of the Fathers declare it to be the demon
of noontide which is spoken of in the xcth Psalm.

When this besieges the unhappy mind, it begets aversion

from the place, boredom with one's cell, and scorn and contempt for one's brethren, whether they be dwelling with one or some way off, as careless and unspiritually minded persons. Also, towards any work that may be done within the enclosure of our own lair, we become listless and inert. It will not suffer us to stay in our cell, or to attend to our reading: we lament that in all this while, living in the same spot, we have made no progress, we sigh and complain that bereft of sympathetic fellowship we have no spiritual fruit; and bewail ourselves as empty of all spiritual profit, abiding vacant and useless in this place; and we that could guide others and be of value to multitudes have edified no man, enriched no man with our precept and example. We praise other and far distant monasteries, describing them as more helpful to one's progress, more congenial to one's soul's health. We paint the fellowship of the brethren there, its suavity, its richness in spiritual conversation, contrasting it with the harshness of all that is at hand, where not only is there no edification to be had from any of the brethren who dwell here, but where one cannot even procure one's victuals without enormous toil. Finally we conclude that there is no health for us so long as we stay in this place, short of abandoning the cell wherein to tarry further will be only to perish with it, and betaking ourselves elsewhere as quickly as possible.

Towards eleven o'clock or midday it induces such lassitude of body and craving for food, as one might feel after the exhaustion of a long journey and hard toil, or the postponing of a meal throughout a two or three days fast. Finally one gazes anxiously here and there, and sighs that no brother of any description is to be seen approaching: one is for ever in and out of one's cell, gazing at the sun as though it were tarrying to its setting: one's mind is in an irrational confusion, like the earth befogged in a mist, one is slothful and vacant in every spiritual activity, and no remedy, it seems, can be found for this state of siege than a visit from some brother, or the solace of sleep. Finally our malady suggests that in common courtesy one should salute the brethren, and visit the sick, near or far. It dictates such offices of duty and piety as to seek out this relative or that, and make haste to visit them; or there is that religious and devout lady, destitute of any support from her family, whom it is a pious act to visit now and then and supply in holy wise with necessary comforts, neglected and despised as she is by her own relations: far better to bestow one's pious labour upon these than sit without benefit or profit in one's cell. . . .

The blessed Apostle, like a true physician of the spirit . . . busied himself to prevent the malady born of the spirit of accidie. . . . *"Study to be quiet . . . and to do your own business . . . and to work with your own hands, as is commended you."* . . .

And so the wise Fathers in Egypt would in no way suffer the monks, especially the younger, to be idle, measuring the state of their heart and their progress in patience and humility by their steadiness at work; and not only might they accept nothing from anyone towards their support, but out of their own toil they supplied such brethren as came by, or were from foreign parts, and did send huge stores of victuals and provisions throughout Libya, a barren and hungry land, and to those that pined in the squalor of the prisons in the towns. . . . There was a saying approved by the ancient Fathers in Egypt; that a busy monk is besieged by a single devil: but an idle one destroyed by spirits innumerable.

So when the abbot Paul, revered among the Fathers, was living in that vast desert of Porphyrio secure of his daily bread from the date palms and his small garden, and could have found no other way of keeping himself (for his dwelling in the desert was seven days journey and more from any town or human habitation, so that more would be spent in conveying the merchandise than the work he had sweated on would fetch), nevertheless did he gather palm leaves, and every day exacted from himself just such a measure of work as though he lived by it. And when his cave would be filled with the work of a whole year, he would set fire to it, and burn each year the work so carefully wrought: and thereby he proved that without working with his hands a monk cannot endure to abide in his place, nor can he climb any nearer the summit of holiness: and though necessity of making a livelihood in no way demands it, let it be done for the sole purging of the heart, the steadying of thought, perseverance in the cell, and the conquest and final overthrow of accidie itself.

2. Of Mortification

The abbot Abraham . . . was silent for a long while, and then with a heavy sigh, at last he spoke. . . .

"We could have built our cells in the valley of the Nile, and had water at our door, nor been driven to bring it to our mouths from three miles off. . . . We are not ignorant that in our land there are fair and secret places, where there be fruit trees in plenty and the graciousness of gardens, and the richness of the land would give us our daily bread with very little bodily toil. . . . But we have despised all these and with them all the luxurious pleasure of the world: we have joy in this desolation, and to all delight do we prefer the dread vastness of this solitude, nor do we weigh the riches of your glebe against these bitter sands. . . . It is a little thing that a monk should have made a single renunciation, that is, in the first days of his calling to have trampled on things present, unless he persist in renouncing them daily. Up to the very end of this life the word of the

Prophet must be in our mouths: *'And the day of man Thou knowest I have not desired.'* Whence the saying of the Lord in the Gospel, *'If any man will come after me, let him deny himself, and take up his cross daily, and follow me.'*

"And so he who keeps an anxious watch over the purity of the inner man will seek those places which have no rich fertility to seduce his mind to their tilling, nor beguile him from his fixed and motionless abiding in his cell to work that is to be done under the sky, whereby his thoughts are emptied out in the open, and all direction of the mind and that keen vision of its goal are scattered over diverse things: and this can be avoided by no man, however anxious and vigilant, save he that shuts in soul and body together within the fence of his walls. Like a mighty fisherman, in the apostle's fashion, perceiving his food in the depths of his most quiet heart, intent and motionless he catches the swimming shoal of his thoughts: and gazing curiously into the depths as from an upstanding rock, judges what fish a man may wholesomely draw in, and which he may pass by or throw out, as bad and poisonous. . . .

"What difficulty and labour there be in this, the experience of those that dwell in the desert of Calamus or Porphyrio doth manifestly prove. For they are divided from all towns and habitations of men by a vaster stretch of desert than even Scete is (for hardly in seven or eight days may those who penetrate the wastes of that vast solitude come at the secret of their cells), nevertheless because they be tillers of the ground and confined in no cloister, when they come to the desolation amid which we live, or to that of Scete, they are harried by such tempests of imagination, by such perturbation of spirit, that they seem to be raw and unskilled in the lightest practises of solitude, and cannot endure the long tarrying in their cell and the stillness of the silence. For they have not learned to quiet the stirrings of the inner man and to beat up against the tempest of their thoughts with perpetual watchfulness and persevering intentness, these that sweat daily at work under the open heavens, all day under the windy emptiness, flitting hither and thither not only in body but in mind, and their thoughts scattering with the movement of their bodies over the open fields. They feel the many-winged folly of their soul, nor can they control its wanton forays: contrition of spirit comes hard to them, they find the perpetual silence intolerable, and these that no labour on the land could weary are vanquished by idleness and worn out by the long lasting of their peace."

FRAGMENTS FROM THE
PARADISUS OF PALLADIUS

from the Greek by an unknown translator

In the year 420, about the time that Cassian was writing his memories of the Desert Fathers, Palladius, now bishop of Helenopolis, was busy with his own.[1] They covered much the same period—the last ten years of the fourth century—but have little else in common. For Palladius took the short view: he is nearer his own Apollonius, in and out of every door with pomegranates and raisins and eggs, than the Fathers of whom he spoke with bated breath. For Melania who so honestly told this story against herself, he had a deep admiration; so had a saintlier and more discriminating judge, Paulinus of Nola.[2] She was a Spaniard, daughter of a consul and widow at twenty-two of a Roman of vast wealth; came on pilgrimage to Egypt; braved the Arian persecution with a courage so indifferent that it seemed like arrogance; and fought like a lioness with her wealth and her prestige for the Fathers who were meeting their enemies with a different kind of courage. The persecutors come into the desert, says Rufinus, horse and foot, tribunes and prefects and captains, to make war on quiet men. "And when they had come there, they found a new kind of fighting: enemies that bowed their necks to the sword, and said nought else but this, *Friend, wherefore art thou come?*"[3] When the troubles were ended, she and Rufinus came together to Jerusalem; Jerome called her "the nobleness of our time."[4] But this was before he quarrelled with Rufinus; after that, he muttered comminations. Yet not even Jerome spoke a word of scandal against the love between these two.

FRAGMENTS FROM
THE *PARADISUS* OF PALLADIUS

ii. The blessed Pambo was a dweller in this mountain [Mt. Nitria]. . . . In many and diverse virtues he had the prerogative and palm, but was in this especially memorable, that he made so light of silver and gold that verily he seemed to have fulfilled the Lord's commandment. I had it myself from the worshipful lady Melania, that after she set out from Rome and first reached Alexandria, she heard much of his virtues from Isidore the priest and overseer of the church, and with him as guide came to him in the desert, and offered him three hundred pounds of silver, praying him to accept somewhat of her wealth. "He was sitting there," said she, "and weaving a basket, and he blessed me with a single word saying, 'May God reward thee.' Then he said to his steward, 'Take it carefully, and divide it among all the brethren that are in Libya and the islands, for these monasteries seem more needy that the others.'" He also bade him give none of the money to those in Egypt, because he knew that these parts have abundance of food. So, as she herself told me, she stood on, waiting for some blessing on her gift or some praise; and hearing nothing from him, at last she spoke. "I would have thee know, my lord," says she, "there are three hundred pounds in that casket." But again without looking up he made answer, "He to whom hast offered it, my daughter, has no need to learn its bulk from thee, for He who weighs the mountains in a balance knoweth far better than thou dost what the weight of this silver may be. If indeed it were to me thou didst offer it, thou didst well to tell me: but if not to me, but to that God who we know did not despise but gave most honour to the two mites, hold thy peace and be still."

Now God so ordained it, she said, that a little while after she came to the mountain, this servant of God went to his rest: with no sickness, no fever to weary him, but stitching together a little basket, he slept in peace, in the seventieth year of his age. "A little before the hour that he went out from the world, commending his soul to God, he called me, and as he came to the last finishing of his work, he said to me, undismayed, 'Take this little basket from my hands, for I have naught else to leave thee, to remember me by.' So when his body was wrapped in linen and carried to its grave, I left those solitudes, but that which the holy man left me I keep with me, until my own end."

iii. A certain Apollonius, that had been a merchant and renounced the world, came to live on Mount Nitria: and since he could learn no art, hindered as he was by weight of years, nor could practise the abstinence laid down in Holy Writ, he laid down a rule of continence for himself. For out of his own purse and labour he bought every kind of remedy and food-stuffs in Alexandria, and provided the brethren that were ailing with whatever they needed. You might see him from early morning till the ninth hour traversing up and down through all the monasteries, whether of men or women, in and out of door after door where there were any sick, carrying with him raisins, and pomegranates, and eggs, and fine wheaten flour, especially necessary for the ailing. To such a life for which alone he was adapted, did this servant of Christ devote his old age: nevertheless before his death when he had found another like unto himself, he handed over to him all the paraphernalia of his ministry, entreating him to have the same care of the brethren. And since there be five thousand monks dwelling in the aforesaid mountain, such tendance and comforting is indeed called for, for without it in those desolate places man could not live.

THE *PRATUM SPIRITUALE*
OF JOHN MOSCHUS

translated from the Greek by Ambrose of Camaldoli

John Moschus was a romantic. He called his collection of stories
of the Fathers λειμών, the water-meadow, or green pastures:
and dedicating it to his friend Sophronius the Scholar, he wrote
a little parable of flowering fields in spring, and how colour and
fragrance alike hold the wayfarer from passing on: and how he
has woven him this garland from those unwithering and eternal
fields.[1] The preface was written in Rome, when he knew that he
was near death. But he himself was a monk from the monastery
of Theodosius, in the solitude near Jerusalem, not far from
where the Laura fell into the Cedron. About the year that the
Emperor Maurice was killed, A.D. 602, he set out on a pilgrimage
through Egypt, and finally to Rome, where he died. He had
asked Sophronius if it were possible to bring his body oversea,
and bury it with the Fathers at Mount Sinai, but not if the barbarians were in turmoil to make the journey dangerous.
Sophronius had brought his dead master as far as Ascalon, when
he heard that the Agareni were out: so he brought him to Jerusalem, and buried him in the monastery where he had first renounced the world, in the cave where the Three Wise Men had
lain hidden from the wrath of Herod.[2] He was a lover alike of
men and beasts, and never weary of stories about the goodness
and guilelessness of lions, and the wisdom of the little dog of the

abbot Subena Syrorum. As for Sophronius the Scholar, he was Patriarch of Jerusalem when he died: and a brief poem on Golgotha has set his name in that other unwithering garland, the Greek Anthology.

PRATUM SPIRITUALE
By John Moschus

i. There was a certain old man living in the monastery of the abbot Eustorgius, John by name, whom the holy Elias, archbishop of Jerusalem, would have set over the monastery. But he would not consent, saying, "It is my will to go to Mount Sinai to pray there." The archbishop would have urged him to be made abbot first and then to go where he willed. But when the old man would not agree, he was suffered to leave, promising that when he returned he would take on himself the task of ruling. So after taking leave of the archbishop, he hastened to take the road that he might come to Mount Sinai, and with him he took his disciple. He had forded the Jordan and gone hardly a stone's throw further, when he felt a stiffness coming upon him, and a little while after he was seized by fever. And when the heat of the fever so mounted in him that he could not walk, they found a little cave, and went into it to rest. But since the fever so weakened him that he could not move, in that cave they remained for three days. Then the old man in his sleep saw one standing by him and saying, "Tell me, old man, whither wouldst thou go?" He answered, "To Mount Sinai." And he said, "Do not, I pray thee, go hence." And when he could not persuade the old man, he went away. But the fever besieged the old man closer.

Again the night following the same man in the same garment stood beside the old man, and said, "Why, old man, wilt thou be made to suffer? Hear me, and go not hence." The old man said, "Who art thou?" And he that had appeared to him said, "I am John the Baptist and for this cause I bid thee go no further: for this low cave is greater than Mount Sinai. For here did our Lord Jesus, when He came to visit us, many a time enter in. Promise me therefore that thou wilt make thy dwelling here and I shall speedily give thee back thy health."

And the old man, hearing this, gladly promised that he would abide in that same cave. And straightway he was made whole, and there did abide for the rest of his days. And he made the cave a church, and gathered brethren together. The place is called Sapsas. Beside it on the left is the brook Kerith, to which Elias was sent in the time of the drought, from the other side of Jordan.

ii. In that same place of Sapsas, there dwelt in a cave another old man of so great virtue that he would welcome the lions into his cave with him, and offer them food in his lap: so full of the divine grace was the man of God.

vii. Another old man lived in the same monastery of Turres: and the fathers of the monastery would have made him abbot, for he was a great man and famous for his virtues. But the old man entreated them, saying, "Forgive me, Fathers, and leave me to weep my sins. I have not merit enough to take the cure of souls: it is a business for Fathers great and excellent, Antony, Pachomius, the holy Theodore." But the brethren would not consent and day after day they beseeched him: and the old man seeing himself overpressed by them, said to them, "Suffer me three days to pray, and whatever God shall bid me do, I shall do it." That day was Good Friday: and on the Sabbath, early in the morning, he fell asleep.

ix. In that monastery of Turres there was an old man that was an earnest lover of holy poverty and almsgiving. So one day there came a poor man to his cell asking alms: and since the old man had but one loaf he brought it out and gave it to the poor man. Then said the beggar, "I do not want bread, but I want clothes." And the old man wishing to succour him, took his hand and brought him into the cell. But the beggar seeing naught of any kind in the cell save only the clothes the old man wore, and moved by his great goodness, opened his wallet, and emptied whatever he had in the midst of the cell, saying, "Take these, good father, and I shall ask somewhere else for whatever I need."

xxiv. A certain old man lived in the monastery at Cuziba, of whom the old men of the place told us that when he was in his own village it was his custom if he saw anyone in the village unable through poverty to sow his field, he would go by night, carrying seed with him, and sow the poor man's field, the owner knowing nothing of it. And when he came to the desert and lived in the monastery at Cuziba, he did the same works of compassion. For he would go along the road that leads from the Jordan to the Holy City, carrying bread and water. And if he saw someone growing weary, he would shoulder his load and climb as far as the Holy Mount of Olives, and return again with others by the same road, carrying their burdens as far as Jericho. You might have seen the old man sometimes carrying a huge bundle and sweating under his load: sometimes carrying a youngster on his shoulder; sometimes two. Sometimes he would be sitting patching the broken shoes of some man or woman: he used to carry with him whatever was needed for that task. He would give some a drink of the water that he carried, to others he would give bread; and indeed if he should come on any naked, he would give him the cloak that he wore. It was sweet, to see the old man toiling day after day. And if he found one dead on the road, he would say over him the wonted psalms and prayers, and give him burial.

xxxiv. The Holy City had another patriarch, Alexander by name, so good, merciful and compassionate that when one of his notaries stole his gold and fled in fear to Egypt, to the Thebaid, and in his wandering lost his way and fell among thieves, and was carried off captive to the uttermost parts of Egypt, the good Alexander hearing of it redeemed him, a prisoner in bonds, for eighty-five pieces of silver. And on his return he used him with such kindness and compassion that a certain man of the townsfolk said, "Nothing so profitable, as to sin against Alexander."

cl. The fathers in that same monastery [of the abbot Theodosius, in the desert near Jerusalem] told us of another old man, saying, "There was an old man in this place who died a little while ago, Pardus by name, a Roman. In his younger days he had been a man of consequence. But one day he had gone to Jericho with mules, and while he was in the inn, there was a little lad about, and by the devil's doing a mule struck him with its hoof and killed him, the abbot Pardus knowing nothing of it. But he was sorely distressed for it, and went away into Arnon and became a hermit, forever grieving and saying, 'I have committed murder and as a murderer am I in judgment condemned.' Now there was a lion in that place near the brook. And each day the abbot Pardus would go to the den of the lion, goading and provoking him to rise up and devour him: but the lion did him no manner of hurt. Then the old man, seeing that he made no way, said to himself, 'I shall sleep on the path whereby the lion goes to the river: and when he comes by on his way to drink, he will devour me.' But as he lay, lo in a little while the lion came and as if endowed with reason he leapt over the old man as peaceable as might be, and touched him not at all.

Then was the old man assured that God had remitted his sins and returning again to his monastery, lived in great continence, edifying all men by his example till the day of his death."

clvii. We came, myself and Sophronius the Scholar, to the monastery of Calamon beside the sacred Jordan, to the abbot Alexander, and with him we found two monks from the monastery of Subena Syrorum. They told us this story, saying: "Ten days ago there came one that entertained pilgrims, dispensing alms, and coming to Subiba Besorum, he gave an offering. And then he asked the abbot of the monastery, saying, 'Of thy charity, send word to thy neighbour monastery of Syrorum to come themselves for their offering, and bid them tell the monastery of Charembe to come likewise.' So the abbot sent a brother to the abbot of Subena Syrorum. And the brother made his way thither, and said to the abbot, 'Come to the monastery of Besorum, and send word to the monastery of Charembe to come also.' But the old man made answer, 'Forgive me, my brother, I have no one to send, but of thy perfect charity go thyself and give the message.' Then said the brother, 'I have never gone thither, nor do I know the way.' Then the old man said to his little dog, 'Go with this brother as far as the monastery at Charembe, so that he may give his message.' And the dog went away with the brother, till he brought him in front of the gate of the monastery." And the brothers who told us the story showed us the dog himself: for they had him with them.

clviii. There is by the Dead Sea a mountain called Mardes, exceeding high. In that mountain hermits dwell: but they have a garden at the foot of the mountain about six milestones distant from them round the margin of the sea and there they have a serving man. So if at any time they wish to send for vegetables, they saddle the donkey and say to him, "Go to the garden to the serving man, and bring us vegetables." And he goes off by himself to the gardener, and stands in front of the gate, and knocks upon it with his head. And straightway the gardener comes out and loads him with vegetables, and sends him away with his load. Daily you may see the donkey climbing up and coming down and ministering to the old men, but he will obey no man else.

clxiii. The abbot Alexander, father of the monastery of Calamon beside the Jordan, used to tell this story. "One day I was with the abbot Paul Helladicus in his cave, and behold one came and knocked, and the old man went out and opened the door, and bringing forth bread and peas that had been steeped, set it before him and he ate. Now I thought it might be a pilgrim, and looking through the window, I saw it was a lion. So I said to the old man, 'Tell me, father, why dost thou give him to eat?' And he said to me, 'Because I admonished him to do hurt to none, neither man nor beast, and said to him, "Come every day and I will give thee thy food." And behold this is now the seventh month since he hath come twice in the day and I give him to eat.'

"Again after a few days I went out to him to buy a wine jar from him, for that was the old man's trade, and I said to him, 'What ails thee, Father? How goes it with the lion?' And he said to me, 'Badly.' And I said, 'How?' And he said, 'The other day he came here that I might give him to eat, but I saw his chin stained with blood, and I said to him, "What is this? Thou hast been disobedient to me, and hast eaten flesh. Blessed be God, I shall give thee no more, a devourer of flesh eating the bread of the fathers: begone." But he was unwilling to go away. Then I took a rope, and trebled it, and gave him three blows with it, and he went away.'"

clxvii. The abbot Agathonicus, head of the monastery of our holy father Saba, used to tell, "I went down one day into Ruba, to make my way to the abbot Poemen the solitary. And when I had found him and had told him my thoughts, he sent me when it came to evening into a cave: it was winter, and that night was bitter chill, and I was stiff with the fierceness of the cold. The old man came to me in the morning, and said to me, 'What ails thee, my son?' I said to him, 'Forgive me, Father, but I passed a bitter night with the cold.' He said to me, 'For my part, my son, I felt no cold.' I was mightily astonished to hear it, for indeed he was naked. And I said to him, 'Of thy charity, tell me how it came that thou didst not feel so fierce a frost?' And he said to me, 'There came a lion, and went to sleep beside me, and he kept me warm.'"

THE LIFE OF ST. PELAGIA
THE HARLOT

by James the Deacon, translated from the Greek by Eustochius

Side by side in the *Vitae Patrum* with the lives of Paula and Marina and Euphrosyne, holy virgins and faithful widows, are the lives of the harlots, Thaïs, Pelagia, Mary of Egypt; and on the *Vita S. Thaïsis* Anatole France founded his study of the Nemesis that waits on the absolute denial of the body. It was no new theory. In the fifteenth-century morality of *Wisdom,* Lucifer speaks of the "grete drede" there is in following the contemplative life: where men have wasted themselves by abstinence,

> "Then febyll ther wyttis and fallen to fondnes,
> Sum into despeyer and sum to madnes. . . .
> Who clymyt hye, hys fall grete ys."

Shakespeare saw it and began to work on it in Angelo in *Measure for Measure;* Victor Hugo saw it, in the face of the Archdeacon watching the execution in the Place de Grève. With the end of the nineteenth century came Freud's first study of hysteria, and the release of the raven brood of inhibitions upon mankind—but the creative imagination had outstripped the clinic. *Thaïs,* published in 1890, is the subtlest indictment of asceticism in European literature. "Spirit must brand the flesh that it may live"; but what if the branding become a cancer?

The attack is the deadlier because of its understanding. To

the last there was something in Anatole France of the little boy who was caught stuffing horsehair from the seat of an armchair inside his tiny shirt, so that when he grew up he might write upon his visiting cards, not, like Papa, "Membre de l'Institut," but "Member of the Calendar of Saints." For goodness that did not vaunt itself and was not puffed up, St. Malo preaching to the penguins, Palemon planting his lettuce, the blessed Antony, he had a profound tenderness; and his own old scholars and abbés owe not a little of their charm to the disconcerting innocent shrewdness of the Desert. No man ever made the saints so lovable: his very malice is a caress. But in the *Vita Sanctae Thaïsis* he had the crudest of the *Vitae Patrum,* and in Paphnutius the harshest figure. It is a hard heart that will not soften to Antony talking to the satyr in the desert and eating the dates the good creature brought him, or to old Abraham getting himself up as an elderly military gentleman and leaving his desert for the brothel in the town, to find his little broken niece and bring her home. Paphnutius had a kind of granite greatness at the first: the gaunt figure reasoning of the wrath of God with the loveliest courtesan in Alexandria is well enough. But Paphnutius sealing up his penitent in a doorless cell, and striking down her timid demurrer with a *Digna es,* since the filth would be a match for herself, forbidding her to lift up her polluted hands to God or take His name upon her lips, but only look to the East and say, "Thou who hast created us, have mercy upon me," is a figure for the vengeance of God and man. Three years later he came and took her from her foul prison, though she clung to it; in a fortnight she was dead. It is a revolting story, and a credit to Anatole France that his gorge rose at it.

But on the next page was the *Vita S. Pelagiae,* the makings of a greater novel than *Thaïs;* and he passed it by. Perhaps the confession of the great Bishop, "Tempt not my weakness, for I am a sinful man, serving God," disarmed him; perhaps he recognised it, in James the Deacon's telling of it, as already a masterpiece, and left it untouched. Of author and translator—James the Deacon, who wrote the Greek original, Eustochius, who turned it into Latin—nothing is known; of Nonnus, Bishop of Edessa, the hero of the story to James, very little, beyond his signature to a few conciliar documents. In 449, in a council at Ephesus, very odd charges were brought against Iba, then Bishop of Edessa, ranging from the disappearance of a jewelled chalice and the ordination of a restless [*inquietum*] and dissolute young man, to the Nestorian heresy and his providing of inferior and muddy wine for the Eucharist. Iba, then absent, was deposed,[1] and the see forced upon the reluctant Nonnus, brought to Syria from his monastery at Tabenna. Two years later, in 451, the Council of Chalcedon dismissed the charges and reinstated Iba, the roar of whose speech vibrates to this day through all the muting of ecclesiastical reporting.[2] The regard of the Council for Nonnus, forced into a position so ungracious, is no less apparent: to call a bishop *"Amantissimus Dei,"* a great lover of God, was almost Byzantine common form, but when they spoke of Nonnus, they added the word *nimirum,* beyond question; he was maintained in the episcopal dignity, and commended to Maximus, patriarch of Antioch.[3] Six years later, Iba, who was an old man, died, and Nonnus, who seems to have served Maximus in the interval as a kind of Minister without Portfolio, was reinstated in Edessa. His name appears in the earlier conciliar documents at Chalcedon with the other bishops of Syria and Mesopotamia.[4] It is curious to reflect that behind some of those signatures, Gerontius of Seleucia, Macarius of Laodicæa, Rufinus of Samosate, Stephen of Hierapolis, Polycarp of Gabala, John, Bishop of the Saracens, Julian of Rhossus, Miletius of Larissa, are the men who saw Pelagia ride by, "bare of head and shoulder and limb . . . in beauty beyond all wearying," and groaned and turned away their heads, as at great and grievous sin; and behind the signature of Edessa, the one man who followed her with his eyes as far as he could see. "Did not the sight of so great beauty delight you? For it greatly delighted me."

The story was written to be read aloud to the brethren, as it might be in the refectory, and James begs for silence, it being, he says, a story of deep repentance and of great consolation. And so, after his little conventional preface, he begins, and already in the first paragraph one knows oneself in the hands of a great novelist. Here is nothing of the wealthy or humble parentage of the saint, her nurture in godliness, her fall from grace. There is no mention of the saint at all; it is a page out of any ecclesiastic's diary. It is not conscious art. James, *diaconus et peccator,* knew no more that he told a great story than he knew that he and his master had once seen Absolute Beauty, and went the rest of their lives the poorer and the richer for it. But he felt sincerely, this small obscure ecclesiastic, trotting in the shadow of his great bishop, and he told the story even as it happened to himself, so that the reader shares his own astonishment and perplexity and ecstasy.

This version of the *Vita* ends with the death of the silent hermit on the Mount of Olives, the finding of the body by James, the discovery at the anointing that it was a woman, and the great company with candles and torches that carried Pelagia to her grave. There is another anonymous translation that adds a single sentence; how James came back to Antioch, and told it all to the lady Romana, and to "my master Nonnus," and how he realised then that Nonnus had always known.[5] Some things James the Deacon never realised: the reason why his sober ecclesiastic's prose goes on fire when he speaks of her, or the lightening of his spirit at his last sight of her. But he at any rate recorded the

things that he did not understand; the harshness of his bishop
with his penitent; her sudden flight in the tunic and cloak of the
blessed Nonnus; the swift closing of the shutter; the one curt
message. If Pelagia had seen the light of the knowledge of the
glory of God in the face of a man, and denied herself the sight
of the one lest she should lose the vision of the other, she kept
her secret; and Nonnus, after that first impulsive pæan to the
Beauty which should judge him and his episcopate, and his
stern confession of his weakness and her power held his peace.
He died, Bishop of Edessa, on December 2nd of some year unknown.

> *Requiescant a labore*
> *Doloroso et amore,*

these to whom religion was not the mask of desire, but the countenance of that eternity which doth ever besiege our life.

THE LIFE OF SAINT PELAGIA THE HARLOT
The Author's Preface

We ought ever to return great thanks to our Lord who desireth
not that sinners should perish in death, but would have all men
turn in penitence to life. Hear therefore the miracle that was
wrought in our time. It seemed good to me, James the sinner, to
write to you, holy brethren, that ye might come to know it, either by listening or reading, and might lay hold on so mighty a
consolation for your souls. For God the merciful, who will have
no man perish, hath decreed that sins may be atoned for in this
world, since in that which is to come there shall be a just Judgment, wherein every man shall receive according to his works.

Now, therefore, give me silence, and look on me with all the intent of your hearts, for my story is of a rich repentance.

The Life

The most venerable bishop of Antioch convened all such bishops as were his near neighbours to confer with him on a certain question: whence it came about that eight bishops assembled, among whom was that saintly man of God, my own bishop, Nonnus, a man marvellous great and a mighty monk of the monastery called Tabenna: but by reason of his rare and gracious way of life, he had been reft from the monastery and ordained a bishop. Come together as we were in the aforenamed city, the bishop thereof appointed us our lodging in the basilica of the blessed Julian the Martyr. We entered, and followed to where the other bishops sat, in front of the door of the basilica.

And as we sat, certain of the bishops besought my master Nonnus that they might have some instruction from his lips: and straightway the good bishop began to speak to the weal and health of all that heard him. And as we sat marvelling at the holy learning of him, lo! on a sudden she that was first of the actresses of Antioch passed by: first of the dancers was she, and riding on an ass: and with all fantastic graces did she ride, so decked that naught could be seen upon her but gold and pearls and precious stones: the very nakedness of her feet was hidden under gold and pearls: and with her was a splendid train of young men and maidens clad in robes of price, with torques of gold about their necks. Some went before and some came after her: but of the beauty and the loveliness of her there could be no wearying for a world of men. Passing through our midst, she filled the air with the fragrance of musk and of all scents that are sweetest. And when the bishops saw her so shamelessly ride by, bare of head and shoulder and limb, in pomp so splendid, and not so much as a veil upon her head or about her shoulders, they groaned, and in silence turned away their heads as from great and grievous sin.

But the most blessed Nonnus did long and most intently regard her: and after she had passed by still he gazed and still his eyes went after her. Then, turning his head, he looked upon the bishops sitting round him. "Did not," said he, "the sight of her great beauty delight you?"

They answered him nothing. And he sank his face upon his knees, and the holy book that he held in his good hands, and his tears fell down upon his breast, and sighing heavily he said again to the bishops, "Did not the sight of her great beauty delight you?"

But again they answered nothing. Then said he, "Verily, it greatly delighted me, and well pleased was I with her beauty: whom God shall set in presence of His high and terrible seat, in judgment of ourselves and our episcopate."

And again he spoke to the bishops. "What think you, beloved? How many hours hath this woman spent in her chamber, bathing and adorning herself with all solicitude and all her mind on the stage, that there may be no stain or flaw in all that body's beauty and its wearing, that she may be a joy to all men's eyes, nor disappoint those paltry lovers of hers who are but for a day and tomorrow are not? And we who have in heaven a Father Almighty, an immortal Lover, with the promise of riches eternal and rewards beyond all reckoning, since eye hath not seen nor ear hath heard nor hath it ascended into the heart of man to conceive the things that God hath prepared for them that love Him—but what need is there of further speech? With such a promise, the vision of the Bridegroom, that great and splendid and ineffable face, whereon the Cherubim dare not look, we adorn not, we care not so much as to wash the filth from our miserable souls, but leave them lying in their squalor."

And with that, he laid hold on me, deacon and sinner, and we made our way to the hospice, where a cell had been given us. And going into his own chamber, he flung himself on the paved floor, his face to the ground; and beating his breast he began to weep, saying, "Lord Christ, have mercy on a sinful man and an unworthy, for a single day's adorning of a harlot is far beyond the adorning of my soul. With what countenance shall I look upon Thee? Or with what words shall I justify myself in Thy sight? I shall not hide my heart from Thee, Thou knowest its secrets. Woe is me, worthless and sinful that I am, for I stand at Thy altar, and offer not the fair soul that Thou askest. She hath promised to please men, and hath kept her word: I have promised to please Thee, and through my sloth have lied. Naked am I in heaven and in earth, for I have not done Thy bidding. My hope is not in any good thing that I have done, but my hope is in Thy pity, whereto I trust my salvation." Such was his prayer and such his lamenting: and vehemently did we keep the fast that day.

But on the day following, which was a Sunday, after we had finished Nocturne, the good bishop Nonnus spoke to me. "I tell thee, brother deacon, I had a dream and am mightily disturbed by it, for I cannot make sense of it." And then he told me how he had seen in his sleep a black dove, standing at the horn of the altar, stained and soiled with filth: "it kept flying round me, and I could hardly bear the stink and squalor of it. But still it kept about me, till the prayer for the catechumens was ended. And then, after the deacon had pronounced the *Procedite,* it was no more seen. But after the mass for the faithful was said and the oblation, and the congregation dismissed, and I crossing the threshold of the House of God, again came that dove in all its squalor, and again it flew about me. But I stretched out my hand and caught it and plunged it into the stoup of holy water in the porch of the church: and it left all the filth that had clung to it in the water and rose out of the water as white as snow: and flying upwards was borne into the high air and vanished from my sight." He finished telling me his dream, Nonnus, God's good bishop, and then took me with him and we came to the greater church with the other bishops and greeted the bishop of the city.

And going in, he spoke to all the clergy of the church, sitting there in their stalls: and after celebration and the reading of the Holy Gospel, the same bishop of the city, handing the Holy Gospel to the blessed Nonnus, begged him to speak to the people. And he spoke to them the wisdom of God that dwelt in him, with no alloy of artifice or of philosophy, naught unfitting, naught of human vanity: but full of the Holy Ghost, he reasoned with and admonished the people, speaking from his heart of the judgment to come and the eternal blessedness that is in store. And so stirred were all the people by the words which the Holy Ghost spake through him that the pavement of the church was wet with their tears.

Now it befell, by the guiding of the Divine compassion, that to this very church should come that harlot of whom he had spoken to us: and for a marvel, she to whom never had come a thought of her sins and who never had been inside a church door was suddenly stricken with the fear of God, as the good Nonnus reasoned with the people: and despairing of herself she fell to sorrowing, her tears falling in streams, and she in no way able to check her weeping. There and then she gave orders to two of her youths, saying, "Stay in this place: and when the good bishop Nonnus comes out, follow him and ask where he lodges and come and tell me." The young men did as their lady had bidden them: they followed us and came to the basilica of the blessed Julian the Martyr, where was our hospice or cell. And then they went back to their lady and said, "He is lodging in the basilica of the blessed Julian the Martyr." Upon this, she straightway sent a diptych by the same two, on which these words were written:

"To Christ's holy disciple, the devil's disciple and a woman that is a sinner. I have heard of thy God, that He bowed the heavens and came down to earth, not for the good men's sake, but that He might save sinners, and that He was so humble that He drew near to publicans, and He on whom the Cherubim dare not look kept company with sinners. And thou my lord, who art a great saint, although thou hast not looked with the eyes of the flesh on the Lord Christ Himself, who showed Himself to that Samaritan woman, and her a harlot, at the well, yet art thou a worshipper of Him, for I have heard the talk of the Christians. If indeed thou art a true disciple of this Christ, spurn me not, desiring through thee to see the Saviour, that through thee I may come at the sight of His holy face."

Then the good bishop Nonnus wrote back to her: "Whatsoever thou art is known unto God, thyself, and what thy purpose is, and thy desire. But this I surely say to thee, seek not to tempt my weakness, for I am a man that is a sinner, serving God. If in very deed thou hast a desire after divine things and a longing for goodness and faith, and dost wish to see me, there are other bishops with me: come, and thou shalt see me in their presence: for thou shalt not see me alone."

She read it, this harlot, and filled with joy came hurrying to the basilica of the blessed Julian, and sent word to us that she was come. On hearing it, the good Nonnus called to him all the bishops who were in the place, and bade her come to him. She came in where the bishops were assembled, and flung herself on the pavement and caught the feet of the blessed Nonnus, saying, "My lord, I pray thee to follow thy master the Lord Christ, and shed on me thy kindness and make me a Christian. My lord, I am a sea of wickedness and an abyss of evil. I ask to be baptised."

Hardly could the good bishop Nonnus prevail on her to rise from his feet: but when she had risen, "The canons of the Church," he said, "provide that no harlot shall be baptised, unless she produce certain to go surety for her that she will not fall back into her old sins."

But on hearing such a judgment from the bishop, she flung herself again on the pavement and caught the feet of the good Nonnus, and washed them with her tears and wiped them with her hair, crying, "Thou shalt answer to God for my soul and on thee shall I charge all the evil of my deeds, if thou dost delay to baptise me in my foul sin. No portion mayst thou find in God's house among the saints, if thou makest me not a stranger to my sin. Mayst thou deny God and worship idols, if thou dost not this day have me born again, bride to Christ, and offer me to God."

Then all the bishops and clergy, who were there gathered, seeing her that was so great a sinner uttering such words in her desire after God, said in wonderment that they had never seen such faith and desire for salvation as in this harlot. And straightway they sent me, deacon and sinner, to the bishop of the city to explain the matter and beg his sanctity to send back one of his deaconesses with me. And when he heard me, he rejoiced mightily, saying, "Verily, father revered, such work as this awaited thee: I know that thou wilt be as my mouth." And he sent with me the lady Romana, chief of the deaconesses.

Coming in, she found her still at the feet of the good bishop Nonnus, and hardly could he persuade her to rise from his feet, saying, "Daughter, arise, that thou mayest be shriven." And then he said to her, "Confess all thy sins."

She made answer, "If I were to search my whole heart I could find in myself no good thing. I know my sins, that they are heavier than the sand of the sea: the waters of it are too scant for the mass of my sin. But I trust in thy God, that He will loosen the load of my wrongdoing, and will look upon me."

Then said the good bishop Nonnus, "Tell me thy name." She answered, "My own name was Pelagia, that my father and mother gave me: but the townsfolk of Antioch call me Margarita, because of the pearls wherewith they did jewel my sins. For I was the devil's jewel and his armoury." Then the good bishop Nonnus again asked her, "Thine own name is Pelagia?" She answered, "Yea, lord."

And thereupon the good bishop exorcised and baptised her, and set upon her the sign of the Cross, and gave her the Body of Christ. Her godmother was the holy lady Romana, chief of the deaconesses: and she took her and went to the place for the catechumens, for so long as we should remain there. Then said to me the good bishop Nonnus, "I tell thee, brother deacon, let us rejoice today with the angels of God, and take oil beyond our custom in our food, and drink wine with joy of heart, for the salvation of this girl."

But as we were at our meal, there came suddenly the sound of shouting as of a man to whom violence is done: it was the devil crying out, "Woe is me, for the things I suffer from this decrepit old man! Might not the thirty thousand Saracens have been enough for thee, that thou didst wrest from me and baptise, and offer to thy God? Might not Heliopolis have been enough for thee, that was mine and all the people in it worshipping me, and thou didst wrest it from me, and offer it to thy God? And now thou hast stolen my greatest hope, and no longer can I endure thy machinations. O the evil this accursed wretch hath wrought upon me! Cursed be the day in which thou wast born! Rivers of tears are flooding my poor house, for my hope is lost!" All this did the devil shout aloud, lamenting up and down outside the gate, and all men heard him. And again he would come and cry out to the girl, "Hast thou done this to me, my lady Pelagia, and dost thou follow my own Judas? For he, crowned with glory and honour and appointed an apostle, betrayed his Master, and so hast thou done to me." Then said to her the good bishop Nonnus, "Sign thyself with the Cross of Christ and renounce him." So she signed herself in the name of Christ, and breathed upon the demon, and straightway he was no more seen.

Two days after, when she was asleep with her godmother the holy lady Romana in her chamber, the devil appeared by night and wakened Pelagia, God's handmaid, and said, "Tell me, my lady Margarita, wert not thou rich in silver and gold? Did I not deck thee with gold and precious stones? Tell me, did I do aught to displease thee? Tell me, that I may make thee amends, but make me not a mock to the Christians." Then Pelagia crossed herself and breathed upon the demon and said, "My God, who snatched me from thy jaws and brought me to His heavenly couch, Himself shall fight thee for me." And straightway the devil vanished.

Now three days after the holy Pelagia had been baptised, she called to her the youth who had had charge of her house, and said to him, "Go to my tiring-room and make a list of everything that is there, gold or silver, or ornaments, or rich apparel, and bring them to me." The boy did as his lady bade him, and brought her all her substance. Then she asked the holy bishop Nonnus to come to her, sending word through her god-mother, the lady Romana, and laid all her substance in his hands, saying, "These, my lord, are the riches wherewith Satan endowed me: I give them to thee to do with as thou wilt, and what seems good to thee, that do: for it is the riches of the Lord Christ that I am fain of now." The bishop straightway summoned the senior treasurer of the church, and in her presence handed over to him all her substance, saying, "I adjure thee, by the indivisible Trinity, that naught of this shall go to the episcopal treasury or to the church, but rather be allotted to the widows and orphans and the poor, so that what was gotten together by ill may be dispersed to good, and the wealth of a sinner become the treasury of righteousness. But if, in contempt of thine oath, aught of this be stolen, let a curse enter either by thee or by some other, whosoever he be, into his house, and let his portion be with those who said, 'Crucify Him; crucify Him.'" But she for her part called together all her young men and her maids, and gave them all their freedom: and with her own hand she gave them golden torques, saying, "Haste ye to set yourselves free from this worthless and sinful world, so that as we were together in this life, so might we abide together without sorrow in that life which is most blessed."

But on the eighth day, when she must lay aside her white robes, she rose by night, without our knowledge, and laid aside the robe of her baptism, and put on the tunic and cloak of the good bishop Nonnus: and from that day she was no more seen in the city of Antioch. The holy Romana used to weep for her with bitter tears, but the good Nonnus would comfort her, saying, "Weep not, daughter, but rejoice rather with great joy, for Pelagia hath chosen the better part, even as Mary, whom the Lord put before Martha in the Gospel." But she went to Jerusalem and built herself a cell in the Mount of Olives, where Our Lord prayed.

And after some time the bishop of the city called all the bishops together, to dismiss them each to his own place. And after a space of three or four years I, James the Deacon, took a great longing to set out to Jerusalem that I might there adore the resurrection of our Lord Jesus Christ, and I asked my bishop if he would give me leave to go. And while giving me leave, he said to me, "I tell thee, brother deacon, when thou dost reach Jerusalem, inquire there for a certain brother Pelagius, a monk and a eunuch, who has lived these many years shut up and in solitude, if so be thou mightst visit him: for thou mightst well profit by him." And all the time he spoke of God's handmaid Pelagia, but I knew it not.

So then, I arrived in Jerusalem, and I adored the holy resurrection of our Lord Jesus Christ: and the next day I made inquiry for this servant of God. And I made my way and found him in the Mount of Olives, where the Lord prayed, in a little cell closed in on every side, and it had a little window in the wall. And I knocked on the shutter of the little window, and straightway she opened to me, and she knew me: but I knew her not. And how could I know her, when she whom I had aforetime seen in beauty beyond all telling was wasted and haggard with fasting? Her eyes were trenches in her face.

"Brother," said she to me, "whence art thou come?" And I answered, "I was sent to thee by the bidding of Nonnus the bishop." Then said she, "Let him pray for me, for he is a saint of God." And therewith she closed the shutter on the window, and began to sing Tierce. And indeed I myself prayed close to the wall of her cell, and went away, much lightened by the angelic vision. And I came back to Jerusalem, and began to go here and there among the monasteries, visiting the brethren.

There was much talk among the monasteries of the fame of the holy Pelagius: and so I made up my mind to go back yet another time to visit him, and be quickened by his salutary speech.

But when I had come again to his cell, and knocked, and even made bold to call upon him by name, there was no answer. I came again and waited a second day, and again a third, now and then calling, "Pelagius!" but I heard no one. So I said to myself, "Either there is no one here, or the monk who was here has gone away." And then, moved by some prompting from God, I said again to myself, "Let me make sure that he is not perhaps dead": and I opened the shutter of the window, and looked in, and I saw him dead. And I closed the shutter and carefully filled it up with clay, and came hurrying to Jerusalem and told the news that the good monk Pelagius who had wrought marvels was at peace. Then the good fathers came with the brethren of divers monasteries, and the door of the cell was opened: and they carried out the holy little body, reckoning it as precious as gold and jewels. And when the good fathers set about anointing the body with myrrh, they found that it was a woman. They would fain have hidden the miracle, but they could not: and they cried aloud with a shout, "Glory to Thee, Lord Christ, who hast many treasures hidden on the earth, and not men only, but women also." It was told abroad to all the people, and all the convents of virgins came, some from Jericho and some from Jordan where the Lord was baptised, with candles and torches and hymns: and so the holy relics of her were buried, and the good fathers carried her to her grave.

This is the story of a harlot, this the life of a desperate sinner: and may God grant that we find with her His mercy in the day of judgment: for to Him is the glory and honour, dominion and power, world without end. Amen.

THE LIFE OF ST. MARY
THE HARLOT

by St. Ephraem of Edessa: translator unknown

"Ephraem, deacon of Edessa," wrote St. Jerome in his catalogue of the Writings of Illustrious Men, "composed many works in Syriac: and he came to such holy renown that in certain churches his writings were read aloud after the lessons from Holy Writ. I myself read a book of his on the Holy Ghost, translated from Syriac into Greek, and even in translation I could recognise the insight of an exalted spirit."[1] He died in 373, a year before Jerome went to the Syrian desert: a little perturbed in his last illness by the threat of a devout lady of his acquaintance that she would have his bones interred in marble, and a similar urn for her own laid ready at his feet; for it seemed to the good old man that posterity might think her his mistress.[2] But he was very gentle with her, very much the "dearest Ephraem" that Abraham speaks of in the text, when he is coaxing his niece to leave the brothel and come home, where the old man is grieving for her. There is no certainty that the two are identical: yet the story is sharp with a personal sorrow, and the whole biography quick with the admiration of a shy man for courage and initiative and power to handle a situation. For Abraham, lover of solitude though he was, had gone from his hermitage to serve as a missionary priest in a pagan city, and after years of persecution and blows had brought the pagans by the sheer obstinacy of his

gentleness to that God whom Ephraem is never weary of calling, "sole Lover of men." A church was founded on the ruins of
a temple, and a community, sufficiently enlightened to go its
own way and provide its own pastors; and one night their priest
prayed God's forgiveness if he were doing wrong, and stole back
to his solitude; "for Thou, who knowest all things, knowest that
I desire none but Thee." How that solitude came to be broken
by a small orphan niece of seven, is the last chapter of his life, as
of his biography.

St. Ephraem was a lover of quiet, said St. Basil:[3] a little, it
would seem, like the Venerable Bede, seldom out of his cell, forever busy with his commentaries, but accessible to any man who
came for teaching: with a kind of blessedness about him.[4] To
himself, he was a poor-spirited creature, who if he had but to say
a word in season to his neighbour, looked forward to it with em-
barrassment and dread.[5] But it so happened that in his old age
there came a cruel famine on the countryside; he saw the peas-
ants dying about him, and their desperation, not his own, drove
him out of his cell. He bearded the rich men of Edessa, asking
them if they had no pity "for human nature dying before your
eyes," or would they keep their rotting wealth intact to the final
damnation of their souls? They paltered with him: they said
that they had no one who could be trusted to lay out the money,
for all men traffic for their private gain. "Ye think so," said he,
"of me?" And with the money he shamed them into giving, the
diffident scholar turned man of affairs, building a rough-and-
ready hospital of three hundred beds, nursing and feeding those
who had any spark of life in them, burying the dead. Another
year came with plentiful harvests, and his salvaged folk went
back to their farms, and there was nothing more for them that
he could do: and suddenly empty-handed, he went back to his
quiet cell and in a month was dead.[6] Winter had indeed come

upon him, the "infinite tempest" had found him, as he thought, naked and spoiled and come to no perfecting; but to his contemporaries it seemed that God's love had given him, as to his other quiet servant Stephen, a sudden glory at his end.[7] He had seen human nature dying before his eyes: and in succouring it, he was to see the taking of the manhood into God.

THE LIFE OF ST. MARY THE HARLOT, NIECE OF THE HERMIT ABRAHAM

The blessed Abraham had a brother after the flesh: and when this brother died, he left behind him an only daughter, a child of seven. Her father's friends and acquaintances, seeing her bereft of her parents, lost no time in bringing her to her uncle. The old man saw her, and had her housed in the outer room of his cell. There was a small window between the two rooms, and through this he taught her the psalter and other passages of Holy Writ, and she kept vigil with him in praising God and would sing the Psalms along with him, and tried to copy her uncle in all abstinence. Eagerly did she seize on this way of life, and made haste to practise all the powers of the soul. And the holy man ceased not to pray with tears, that her mind might not be tangled with the cares of the doings of earth: for her father in dying had left her vast wealth: but the brother being dead, and the daughter taking refuge with him, the servant of Christ gave orders that it should be shared among the poor and the orphaned. She herself would ask her uncle every day to pray God for her, that she might be caught away from evil imaginings and the diverse traps and snares of the devil. And so she steadily followed her rule of life. Her uncle had joy to see her so swift and unhesitant in all good, in tears, in humbleness, in modesty, in quiet: and what is higher than all these, in great devotion towards God. Twenty years she lived with him in abstinence, even as an innocent lamb and an untarnished dove. But by the end of those years, the evil one began to wax violent against her, laying down his wonted snares; for let him once have her webbed in his net, and he could strike grief and anxiety into the holy man and separate some part of his mind at least from God.

Now a certain monk, but a monk in profession only, was in the habit of journeying often to visit the old man, under colour of edification. But gazing on that blessed creature through the window, he was pricked with the goads of lust: he began to long to speak with her, for wanton love had kindled his heart like a fire. For a great while he lay in ambush about her, so that a whole year went by before he had enervated her imagination by the softness of his words. But at the last she opened the window of her cell and came out to him: and forthwith he debauched and defiled her with evil and lust. But when the deed of shame was done, her heart trembled: and tearing the hair shift that clothed her, she began beating her face with her hands, and in her sorrow would have sought for death. Weighed down with anguish she could see no harbour wherein she might tarry and take thought: swayed to and fro on shifting tides of imagination, she wept that she was no longer what she had been, and her speech was broken with wailing. "From this time forward," she said, "I feel as one that has died. I have lost my days and my travail of abstinence, and my tears and prayers and vigils are brought to nothing: I have angered my God, and have destroyed myself. Sorrow upon me, with every spring of tears! I have bowed down that saint my uncle with grief most bitter: shame has gone over my soul: I am become the devil's mock. Why should such as I live on? Sorrow upon me, what have I done? Sorrow upon me, what came upon me? Sorrow upon me, what

evil have I wrought? Sorrow upon me, from what have I fallen?
How was my mind darkened? I know not how I fell, I know not
how I was defiled, I know not what cloud darkened my heart,
how I could be ignorant of what I was doing. Where shall I flee
to hide? Where can I find a pit wherein to throw myself? Where
was my uncle's teaching, and the counsels of Ephraem his
friend, that would urge me to abide in my virginity and keep my
soul unsullied for the immortal Bridegroom? For thy Bridegroom, they would say, is holy and jealous. Sorrow upon me,
what am I to do? I dare not look at heaven, I that am dead to
God and man. I shall not dare now to go near that window.
How could I attempt ever to talk again with my good uncle,
filthy as I am with all uncleanness? If I did, would not a flame
leap from the window and burn me there to ashes? Better to go
away to some other country where there is no one who could
know me, for I am nought but a dead woman now, and there is
no hope left to me anymore." So she rose, and made her way to
another city, and changing the garb of her youth, took refuge in
a certain brothel.

Now at the time that ruin thus befell the maid, a vision came
to the holy man in his sleep. For he saw a huge and monstrous
dragon, most foul in its aspect and strongly hissing: it seemed to
issue from a certain spot and come up to his cell, and there it
found a dove and gulped it down, and again returned to its den.
Wakening in heavy sadness, he began bitterly to weep, for he
judged that Satan had roused up a persecution against the
Church of God and that many were turned from the truth, or
that some schism had been begotten in holy Church. Falling on
his knees, he prayed to God, saying, "Thou that art God fore-
seeing all things, Lover of men, Thou knowest what this vision
may mean." Again after two days he saw the same dragon come
in like fashion to his cell, and it laid its head under its paws and

burst asunder: but that dove which it had devoured was found alive in its belly: and he reached out his hand and took it alive. Waking from sleep, he called that blessed maid once and again, thinking that she was in her cell. "What ails thee, Mary my daughter," said he (for thus was she called), "that for two days thou hast not opened thy mouth in praise to God?" But when there was no answer, and since for two days he had not heard her singing as she was wont to do, he understood that his vision must surely touch her close. Then he sighed and wept sore. "Sorrow upon me," he said, "for a cruel wolf hath stolen my lamb, my daughter is made captive." And lifting up his voice, "Christ," he said, weeping, "Saviour of the world, send Mary my lamb back to me again, and restore her to the fold of life, that my old age go not in sorrow from the world. Despise not my be-seeching, Lord, but be swift to send Thy grace, to cast her forth unharmed from the dragon's mouth." Now the two days which he saw in the vision were measured by the passage of two years, wherein his niece led a wanton life, as in the belly of that mon-strous dragon: but through all that time the saint not once re-laxed his mind by day or night from entreating God for her.

So then, it was two years before he discovered where she was and what she did: and he asked a singular good friend of his to go to the place and find out all he could. The friend set out, and coming again he told him all the truth, and how he himself had seen her: and at the old man's asking, he brought him a military habit, and a horse to ride. So he opened his door, and dressed himself in military garb, and set a great hat upon his head, so as to cover his face: but he also took a gold piece with him, and got up on the horse, and made all haste upon the road. Even as one desirous of spying out a country or a city will put on the garb of its inhabitants lest he be recognised: so did the blessed Abraham make use of the garb of the enemy to put him to rout. Come now, brothers beloved, and marvel at this second Abraham. The first Abraham went forth to do battle with the Kings, and smote them and brought back his nephew Lot: but this second Abraham went forth to do battle with the Evil One, and having vanquished him, bring home again his niece in a greater triumph.

So then, arrived at the town, he stepped aside into the tavern, and with anxious eyes he sat looking about him, glancing this way and that in hopes to see her. The hours went by, and still no chance of seeing her appeared: and finally he spoke jestingly to the innkeeper. "They tell me, friend," said he, "that thou hast a very fine wench: if it were agreeable to thee, I should like well to have a look at her."

The innkeeper regarded the hoary head, the old frame bowed with its weight of years, and in no hope that this desire for a sight of her was prompted by lechery, made reply that it was indeed as he had heard: that she was an uncommon handsome lass. And indeed Mary in beauty of body was fair, wellnigh beyond aught that nature demandeth. The old man asked her name, and was told that they called her Mary. Then, with merry countenance, "Come now," said he, "bring her in and show her to me, and let me have a fine supper for her this day, for I have heard the praises of her on all hands." So they called her: but when she came in and the good old man saw her in her harlot's dress, his whole body wellnigh dissolved in grief. Yet he hid the bitterness of his soul behind a cheerful countenance, and checked by force of his manhood the starting tears, for fear that the girl might recognise him and take flight.

So as they sat and drank their wine, the great old man began to jest with her. The girl rose and put her arms about his neck, beguiling him with kisses. And as she was kissing him, she smelt the fragrance of austerity that this lean body breathed, and remembered the days when she too had lived austere: and as if a spear had pierced her soul, she gave a great moan and began to weep: and not able to endure the pain in her heart, she broke out into words, "Woe's me, that am alone unhappy!"

The innkeeper was dumbfounded. "What ails thee, mistress Mary," said he, "to burst out all of a sudden into this sore lamenting? It is two years today that thou hast been here, and no one ever heard a sigh from thee or a sad word: indeed I know not what has come over thee."

"I had been happy," said the girl, "if three years ago I had died."

At this the good old man, afraid that she might recognise him, spoke to her genially enough. "Now, now!" said he, "here am I come to make merry, art going to begin the tale of thy sins?" Marvellous is the ordering of Thy mercy, O God most high! Thinkest thou the maid did not say in her heart, How comes it that this old man's look is so like my uncle's? But Thou, that are alone the Lover of men, from whom all good wisdom comes, Thou didst order it that she could not recognise him and flee in shame. It would indeed be past belief, were it not that the tears of Thy servant her uncle had come before Thee, so that Thou didst deign out of impossibility to make the possible.

So then, the good old man produced the gold piece he had brought with him and gave it to the innkeeper. "Now friend," said he, "make us a right good supper, so that I may make merry with the lass: for I am come a very long journey for love of her." O wisdom as of God! O wise understanding of the spirit! O memorable discretion in salvation! Throughout fifty years of abstinence he had never tasted bread: and now without a falter eats meat to save a lost soul. The company of the holy angels, rejoicing over the discretion of the blessed man, were mazed at that which he ate and drank, lighthearted and nothing doubting, to deliver a soul sunken in the mire. O wisdom and understanding of the wise! O discrimination of the discerning! Come, marvel at this madness, this reversal, when an upright and wise and discreet and prudent man is made a reckless fool to snatch a soul from the jaws of the lion, and set free a captive bound and thrust away from its chains and its dark prison-house.

So, when they had feasted, the girl began to provoke him to come to her room to lie with her. "Let us go," said he. Coming in, he saw a lofty bed prepared, and straightway sat gaily down upon it. What I shall call thee, O perfect athlete of Christ, I know not. Shall I say that thou art continent or incontinent, wise or foolish, discreet or reckless? For the fifty years of thy profession thou hast slept on a mat of rushes, and how dost thou indifferently climb on such a bed? But all these things thou hast done to the praise and glory of Christ, this long journey of many halting-places, this eating of flesh and drinking of wine, this turning aside to a brothel, to save a lost soul. While for our part, if we have to say but one useful word to our neighbour, we look forward to it all with sore distress.

So then, the girl says to him, as he sits there on the bed: "Come, sir, let me take off your shoes." "Lock the door carefully," said he, "and then take them off." The girl would have taken his shoes off first: but as he would not let her she locked the door and came to him.

"Come close to me, mistress Mary," said the old man. And when she was beside him he took her firmly by the hand as if to kiss her, then taking the hat from his head and his voice breaking into weeping, "Mary, my daughter," said he, "dost thou know me? My heart, was it not I that brought thee up? What has come to thee, my child? Who was it destroyed thee? Where is that angel's garb thou didst wear, my daughter? Where is thy continence, thy tears, thy vigils, thy bed on the ground? How didst thou fall from heaven's height into this pit, my daughter?

Why, when thou didst sin, didst thou not tell me? Why didst thou not come there and then? And indeed I would have done thy penance for thee, and my dear Ephraem too. Why didst thou act like this? Why didst thou desert me, and bring me into this intolerable sorrow? For who is without sin, save God Himself?"

This and much else he said: but all the while she stayed in his hands, motionless as a stone. Fear and shame had filled her full.

And again the old man began, weeping, "Mary, child, wilt thou not speak to me? Will thou not speak to me, half of my heart? Was it not because of thee, my child, that I came here? Upon me be this sin, O my daughter. It is I that shall answer for thee to God at the day of Judgment. It is I that shall give satisfaction to God for this sin." And until midnight he sought to comfort her, with such words as these, encouraging her with many tears. Little by little she took courage, and at last she spoke to him, weeping, "I cannot," she said, "look on your face for shame. And how can I pour out a prayer to God, so foul as I am with the mud of this uncleanness?"

Then said the holy man, "Upon me be thy guilt, my daughter: at my hand shall God requite this sin: do but listen to me, and come, let us go home. For look you, there is our dear Ephraem grieving sore for thee, and for even pleading with God for thee. Be not mistrustful, daughter, of the mercy of God; let thy sin be as mountains, His mercy towers above His every creature. We read that an unclean woman came to Him that was clean, and she did not soil Him, but was herself made clean by Him: she washed the Lord's feet with her tears, and dried them with her hair. If a spark can set on fire the sea, then can thy sins stain His whiteness: it is no new thing to fall in the mire, but it is an evil thing to lie there fallen. Bravely return again to that place from whence thou camest: the Enemy mocked thee falling, but he shall know thee stronger in thy rising. Have pity, I pray thee, on my old age: grieve for the travail of my white head: rise up, I implore thee, and come with me home. Fear not: mortal man is apt to slip: but if he be swift to fall swift is he to rise again with the succour of God who desireth not the death of a sinner, but rather that he be healed and live."

Then she said, "If you are sure that I can do penance and that God will accept my atonement. Behold I shall come as you bid me: go before and I shall follow your goodness and kiss the track of your feet, you that have so grieved for me, that you would draw me out of this cesspit." And laying her head at his feet, she wept all night, saying, "What shall I render to Thee for all this, O Lord my God?"

When dawn had come, the blessed Abraham said to her, "Rise up, daughter, and let us go home to our cell." And answering him, she said, "I have a little gold here, and some clothes, what would you have me do with them?" But the blessed Abraham made answer, "Leave all those things here, for they were earned from the Evil One." And they rose up and went away. And he set her upon his horse and led it, going before, even as the good shepherd when he has found his lost sheep, carries it with joy upon his shoulder: and so the blessed Abraham, with joy in his heart, journeyed along the road with his niece. And when he had come home, he set her in the inner cell which had been his own, and himself remained in the outer. And she, clad in her hair shift, did there abide in humility of soul and in tears from the heart and the eyes, disciplining herself with vigils and stern travail of abstinence, in quiet and modesty unweariedly calling upon God, bewailing her sin but with sure hope of pardon, with supplication so moving that no man, even were he without bowels of compassion, could hear her sorrowful crying and not be stirred. For who so hard-hearted as to know her weeping, and himself not weep? And who but gave God thanks for the true repentance of her heart? Indeed her repentance, compared with such prayers as ours, surpassed all measure of grief. So urgently did she pray God to pardon the thing she had done that she obtained from on high a sign that her penitence was accepted. And God the compassionate, who will have no man perish but that all should come to repentance, so accepted her atonement that after three full years He restored health to many at her prayer. For crowds flocked to her, and she would pray to God for their healing, and it was granted her.

And the blessed Abraham, after living for another ten years in his life, and seeing her blessed penitence, and giving glory to God, rested in peace in the seventieth year of his age. For fifty years in devotion and humility of heart and love unfeigned, he had fulfilled his vow. . . .

And Mary also lived another five years, yet more devoutly ruling her life, and persevering night and day in prayer to God, with lamentation and tears, so that many a one passing that place at night and hearing the voice of her grieving would himself be turned to weeping, and add his tears to hers. But when the hour of her sleeping came, wherein she was taken up from this life, all that saw her gave glory to God, for the splendour of her face.

Sorrow on me, beloved, for these fell on sleep, and with all confidence have gone their ways to God: whose minds were never set upon the business of earth, but on the sole love of God. And I unapt and reluctant in my will abide, and behold winter hath come upon me, and the infinite tempest hath found me naked and spoiled and with no perfecting of good in me.

I marvel at myself, beloved, how I daily default, and daily do repent: I build up for an hour, and an hour overthrows what I have builded. At evening I say, "Tomorrow I shall repent": but when morning comes, joyous I waste the day. Again at evening I say, "I shall keep vigil all night, and I shall entreat the Lord with tears, to have mercy on my sins": but when night has come, I am full of sleep. Behold, those who received their talent along with me strive day and night to trade with I, that they may win the word of praise, and rule over ten cities: but I in my sloth hid mine in the earth, and my Lord makes haste to come; and behold my heart trembles and I weep the days of my negligence and know not what excuse to bring.

Have mercy upon me, Thou that alone art without sin, and save me, who alone art pitiful and kind: for beside Thee, the Father most blessed, and Thine only begotten Son who was made flesh for us, and the Holy Ghost who giveth life to all things, I know no other, and believe in no other. And now be mindful of me, Lover of men, and lead me out of the prison-house of my sins, for both are in Thy hand, O Lord, the time that Thou didst will me to come into this world, and the time that Thou shalt bid me go out from it elsewhere. Remember me that am without defence, and save me a sinner: and may Thy grace, that was in this world my aid, my refuge and my glory, gather me under its wings in that great and terrible day. For Thou knowest, Thou who dost try the hearts and reins, that I did shun much of evil and the byways of shame, the vanity of the impertinent and the defence of heresy. And this not of myself, but of Thy grace wherewith my mind was lit. Wherefore, holy Lord, I beseech Thee, bring me into Thy kingdom, and deign to bless me with all that have found grace before Thee, for with Thee is magnificence, adoration, and honour, Father, Son, and Holy Ghost. Amen.

NOTES

The text is Rosweyde's, in the second revised edition of his *Vitae Patrum,* published at Antwerp in 1628. A more accessible though less accurate edition is to be found in Migne, *Patres Latini,* vols. lxxiii, lxxiv. The references given here are to chapter and section, not to page, and the following abbreviations have been used.

P.L. = Migne, *Patres Latini.*

P.G. = Migne, *Patres Graeci.*

Hist. Mon. = *Historia Monachorum, Vitae Patrum,* II.

Pelagius = *Verba Seniorum,* translated by him. *Vit. Pat. V.*

John the Subdeacon = *Verba Seniorum,* translated by him. *Vit. Pat.* VI.

Paschasius = *Verba Seniorum,* translated by him. *Vit. Pat.* VII.

John Moschus = *Pratum Spirituale,* compiled by him. *Vit. Pat.* X.

Hist. Laus. = *Historia Lausiaca,* translated by Hervetus in the sixteenth century. *Vit. Pat.* VIII.

Paradisus = *Paradisus Heraclidis,* believed to represent the original version of the *Historia Lausiaca* of Palladius: a very ancient translation. *Vit. Pat.* Appendix.

INTRODUCTION

1. *Vita B. Antonii,* lviii, lix (*Vit. Pat.* I).
2. *"acris et ferventis ingenii."* Jerome, *De Vir. Illust.* cxxv.
3. *Vita B. Ant.,* Epilogue and Prologue.
4. *Vita B. Ant.* xv.
5. Augustine, *Conf.* viii, 6, 7, 8.
6. *"Nolite, quæso . . . virtus quæ in nobis est, mentem tantum requirit humanam."* *Vita B. Ant.* xv.
7. *Heraclidis Paradisus,* xix, xx: *ib.* ii: *Paschasius,* xliii, i; *Hist. Mon.* vii.
8. *Hist. Mon.* xxix; Pelagius, xvii, 7; *ib.* ix. 2; *Hist. Mon.* xxii; Pelagius, xvii, 5.
9. Prudentius, *Cont. Symm.* i. 626-637.
10. "O Roma nobilis, orgis et domina,
    cunctarum urbium excellentissima,

[211]

roseo martyrum sanguine rubea
albis et virginum liliis candida. . . ."

See Traube, *O Roma nobilis, Abhand. d. Bayer. Akad.* 1891, 299 f.
11. For biography and text see J. Vessereau, *Claudius Rutilius Namatianus,* 1933. The date of the departure from Rome is the autumn of 419 (*op. cit.,* pp. xii-xv).
De Reditu Suo, ll. 439-452.

Squalet lucifugis insula plena viris. . . .
munera fortunæ metuunt, dum damna verentur.
quisquam sponte miser ne miser esse queat?
quænam perversi rabies tam stulta cerebri,
dum mala formides, nec bona posse pati?
sive suas repetunt factorum ergastula poenas,
tristia seu nigro viscera felle tument.

12. *ib.* ll. 519-526.

Impulsus furiis homines terrasque reliquit,
et turpem latebram credulus exul agit,
infelix putat illuvie cælestia pasci.
seque premit læsis sævior ipse deis,
num, rogo, deterior Circæis secta venenis,
tunc mutabantur corpora, nunc animi.

13. Paulinus of Nola, *Carmina,* x. 162-180; text and translation in *Medieval Latin Lyrics,* p. 34.
14. *Vita S. Simeoni Stylitae.* x (*Vit. Pat.* I).
15. Pelagius, xi, 12.
16. *Heracl. Parad.* 1.
17. Pelagius, viii (*Quod nihil per ostensionem fieri debeat*): *ib.* xviii. 1; Paschasius, xii. 6.
18. *Heracl. Parad.* vi.
19. *"longe asperrima, squalida, et plane arida,"* Hist. Laus., ii.
20. *ib.* xliii.
21. *Vit. Pat.* III, 124.
22. *Sententiae Patrum,* edited by Dom Wilmart, *Le recueil latin des Apophtègmes,* in *Revue Bénédictine,* 1922, pp. 185 ff.
23. Pelagius, xi, 5.
24. *ib.* xvii, 2.
25. *ib.* i, 4: *Vita B. Ant.* xv.

26. *"Quis mihi locum avium poterit ostendere"? Vita B. Ant.* xxiv.

27. Jerome, *Vita B. Pauli,* viii *(Vit. Pat.* I).

28. Theodosius *"filios suos tradidit, non ut imperatores, sed liberorum atque discipulorum loco habendos,"* Migne, *P.G.* lxv, 103, note; Pelagius, ii, 5.

29. Cassian, *Collationes,* xix, 5.

30. Bede, *Vita S. Cudberti,* xvii.

31. Pelagius, x, 33: *ib.* 111.

32. *Hist. Laus.* xx.

33. *Vit. Pat.* III, 195: an anonymous collection, ascribed, but uncertainly, to Rufinus.

34. John the Subdeacon, iii, 2.

35. *Inferno,* xv, 46-51.

36. *Conf.* vii, 23.

37. Cassian, *Collationes,* ix, 25; x, 7; i, 6, 7.

38. *P.L.* xlix, 45-9.

39. Pelagius, xviii. 1.

40. John the Subdeacon, i, 1.

41. Pelagius, xv, 16, 18.

42. Pelagius, x, 39.

43. *ib.* xv, 47.

44. *ib.* xv, 4.

45. *"Et lux inaccessibilis . . . accessum præbuit . . . in ipso omnia visibilia et invisibilia, hoc est sensibilis et intelligibilis mundus, restaurata inque unitatem ineffabilem revocata sunt." De Divisione Natræ,* v. 25 *(P.L.* cxxii, 912).

46. *ib.* v, 38 *(P.L.* cxxii, 1022).

47. *". . . cum humanæ vitæ spatia æternitati comparata brevissima sint et parva." Vita B. Ant.* xv.

48. Paulinus of Nola, *Carm.* xxvii, 301-304; *Medieval Latin Lyrics,* p. 40.

49. *". . . otium sanctum quærit charitas veritatis: negotium iustm suscipit necessitas charitatis."* Augustine, *De Civ. Dei,* xix, 19.

50. *Inferno,* xv, 84-5.

51. Un punto solo m'è maggior letargo
    che venticinque secoli alla impresa
    che fe' Nettuno ammirar l'ombra d'Argo.

    Paradiso, xxxiii, 94-6.

52. Boethius, *De Consolatione Philosophiæ,* v, 6.

THE LIFE OF ST. PAUL THE FIRST HERMIT

Text in the *Vitae Patrum,* I, and in Migne's edition of Jerome, *P.L.* xxiii, 18 ff.

1. See in general the earlier letter of Jerome (Migne, *P.L.* xxii), especially to Florentius (*Epistolae,* v); to Theodosius of Rhossus (*Ep.* ii.; see the account of Theodosius by Theodoret in *Vitae Patrum,* IX, 10); to Rufinus (*Ep.* iii); to Eustochium (*Ep.* xxii); to Heliodorus (*Ep.* xiv); and his *Vita S. Marlchi,* c. 1.

2. Ad Eustochium, *Ep.* xxii, 7.

3. *Tunc me tenebat eremus (et utinam pertenuisset).*
    Ad Pammachium, *Ep.* lxvi, 13.

4. Ad Paulum Concordiæ, *Ep.* x.

5. *Ep.* xxii, 30.

6. Ad Rusticum, *Ep.* cxxv, 12.

7. Ad Damasum, *Ep.* xv, xvi; Ad Marcum, xvii.

8. *De Illust. Vir.,* cxxxv.

9. *Vita S. Malchi,* x.

HISTORY OF THE MONKS OF EGYPT

Text in *Vitae Patrum,* II, and in Migne's edition of Rufinus, *P.L.* xxi, 387 ff.

1. Jerome, *Ep.* iii, 2, 6, Ad Rufinum.

2. *Ep.* cx, 6, 7, 8 (Augustine to Jerome).

3. *Ep.* iv, Ad Florentium.

4. *"glutino charitatis hærentum." Ep.* iii, Ad Rufinum.

5. *Ep.* xxii, 30.

6. Rufinus, *Apologia,* ii, 7 ff. (Migne, *P.L.* xxi).

7. Jerome, *Apologia,* i, 30, 31 (Migne, *P.L.* xxiii).

8. *"omissa omni ironia et tergiversatione quæ Deo execrabilis est."*
    Rufinus, *op. cit.,* 1, 2.

9. *"Dicite eum male sensisse de Filio, peius de Spiritu Sancto ..."*
    Jerome, *Ep.* lxxxiv, 7. Ad Pammachium et Oceanum.

10. *"Tu qui invenis es et in pontificali culmine constitutus, doceto populos et novis Africæ frugibus Romana texta locupleto. Mihi sufficit cum auditore et lectore pauperculo in angulo monasterii susurrare." Ep.* cxii, 22. Ad Augustinum.

11. *Ep.* cxxv. 18, Ad Rusticum.

12. On the *Historia Monachorum,* see Dom Cuthbert Butler, *Historia Lausiaca,* pp. 7 ff., 196 ff., Appendix I.

13. *Vit Pat.* II, Prologus.

14. *Ep.* cxxxiii, 3. Ad Ctesihontem. See note in Migne, *P.L.* xxii, c. 1151.
15. Palladius, *Hist. Laus.* lxxvii-lxxxii.
16. *ib.* cxviii.
17. The story of Gerasimus and his Lion is in John Moschus, *Pratum Spirituale,* c. 107 (*Vit. Pat.* x); of Jerome and his Lion in Migne, *P.L.* xxii, 209 ff. Translations of both in *Beasts and Saints,* 25-38.

THE SAYINGS OF THE FATHERS
Translated by Pelagius

Text in *Vitae Patrum,* V and VI. The original Greek text from which Pelagius and John translated was divided into twenty-two chapters: John began his share of the work in the middle of chapter xviii, and the copyists finally made two books of it. Here the original sequence is kept, for the sake of continuity.

1. H. Brémond, *Les Pères du Désert,* p. 16, in *Divertissements devant l'Arche* (Paris, 1930).
2. J. Lebreton, *Bulletin d'histoire des origines chrétiennes* in *Recherches de Science Religieuse,* 1924, pp. 358-363.
3. Jerome, *Ep.* vii, 2.
4. *Vita S. Arsenii* (c. 354-450); *Acta Sanctorum,* July 19, pp. 618 ff.
5. *Hist. Mon.* vi.
6. Pelagius, xiv, 5.
7. Jerome, *Ep.* cxxxiii, 3, Ad Ctesihontem.
8. Pelagius, xv, 7. Cf. *ib.* x, 76, which is definitely ascribed to Arsenius in the *Apophthegmata* (Migne, *P.G.* lxv, 102).
9. *Apophthegmata Patrum* (Migne, *P.G.* lxv).
10. Jerome, *Ep.* xiv, 10, Ad Heliodorum.
11. *Vitae Patrum,* Prolegomena, xiv. See Wilmart, "Le recueil latin des Apophtegmes," *Revue Bénédictine,* 1922, 185 ff.
12. "*Præceptoris mei Donati.*" *Apol. ad Ruf.* i. 16.
13. Paradisus, ii; *Hist. Mon.* xxii, xxix; Wallis Budge, *Paradise of the Fathers,* pp. xvi, xviii.
14. Pelagius, xi, 19. The remaining references are only to such stories as are not contained in the present collection.
15. Cassian, *Collationes,* i. 23.
16. *Vita S. Pachomii,* ix, xi (*Vit. Pat.* I).
17. *Vita B. Antonii,* xxiv, xxv; Cassian, *Collationes,* xxiv, 12.

18. Sulpicius Severus, *Dialogus,* i, 14; Pelagius, xiii, 15.
19. Compare the saying of Ciaran of Clonmacnoise: "Leave my bones as it might be the dry bones of a stag on the mountain."
20. John the Subdeacon, Book I. i *(Vit. Pat.* VI).
21. John the Subdeacon, Book III.
22. The gap in John's text is supplied from the version in *Vit. Pat.* III, 172.
23. John the Subdeacon, Book IV.

THE SAYINGS OF THE FATHERS
By an unknown translator
Text in *Vitae Patrum,* III, there ascribed to Rufinus.

1. *Vit. Pat.* Prolegomena v.
2. Cf. *infra* xxiv and xxvi with *Hist. Mon.* xvi.
3. Cf. *infra* lxxvii, Pelagius, xvi, 10; *infra* v, Pelagius, x. 97; *infra* cxxiv, Pelagius, xv, 26; *infra* lxx, Pelagius, vi, 5.
4. *Infra,* cxxxii.

THE SAYINGS OF THE FATHERS
Translated by Paschasius
1. Gregory of Tours, *Historia Francorum,* v, 38.
2. Fortunatus, *Carmina,* v, 1, 2.
3. Mansi, *Concilia,* ix, 846. "Since it is difficult to make even a simple translation of anything from one language into another, and since it also happens that in so great passage of time the writers, either from lack of comprehension or drowsiness, pass over many things," he has endeavoured to restore the text *simplicius et emendatius,* to something of its original forthright integrity.
4. *Vita S. Martini Dumiensis. Acta Sanctorum,* March 20, 86 ff.
5. *Vit. Pat.* Prolegomena xxiv.

OF ACCIDIE: OF MORTIFICATION
By Cassian of Marseilles
Text from the Migne edition of Cassian, *P.L.* xlix; *Of Accidie,* in *De Cænobiorum Institutis,* x, 1, 2, 7, 22, 24; *Of Mortification,* in *Collationes,* xxiv, 1, 2, 3, 4.

1. "huc de Bethleemitici coenobii rudiments . . . properavimus." *Coll.* xi, 5.
2. Migne, *P.L.* xlix, 53.
3. *ib.* 56.

4. *ib.* 60.
5. *Coll.* xxiv, 1.

FRAGMENTS FROM THE *PARADISUS* OF PALLADIUS

Text in *Paradisus Heraclidis,* chapters ii, iii (*Vit. Pat.* Appendix).

1. E. C. Butler, *Historia Lausiaca,* pp. 179 ff.
2. Paulinus of Nola, *Epist.* xxix (*P.L.* lxi, 315 ff).
3. Rufinus, *Hist. Eccl.* ii, 3 (Migne, *P.L.* xxi, 511).
4. "Sancta Melania nostri temporis . . . nobilitas." Jerome, *Epist.* xxxix, 4, Ad Paulam.

THE *PRATUM SPIRITUALE OF* JOHN MOSCHUS

Text in *Vitae Patrum,* x.

1. *Vit. Pat.* x. Prologus Sophronio.
2. *ib. Elogium Auctoris:* Prolegomena xii.

THE LIFE OF ST. PELAGIA THE HARLOT

Text in *Vitae Patrum,* I.

1. For the "Thieves' Kitchen" of Ephesus (Pope Leo called it the "Latrocinium"), see Mansi, vi, 503-504; for the charges against Iba, *ib.* vii. 222-227.
2. Mansi, vii, 267-270.
3. *ib.* vii, 262-263.
4. *ib.* vi, 566 ff., 938-978.
5. *Acta SS.* Oct. 8., *Vita S. Pelagiæ,* p. 268.

THE LIFE OF ST. MARY THE HARLOT

Text in *Vitae Patrum,* I. See also the *Vita S. Abraham, ib.*

1. Jerome, *De Vir. Illust.* cxv.
2. *Opera S. Ephraem* (Caillau, *Patres IV Sæculi*), vol. iii, pp. 171-172 (*Testamentum,* 133-134).
3. *Vita S. Ephraem,* c. vi *(Vit. Pat. I).*
4. *Paradisus Heraclidis,* c. xxviii.
5. *infra,* p. 297.
6. *Paradisus Heraclidis,* c. xxviii.
7. *ad exemplum Stephani . . . ib.* cxxviii.

SUGGESTIONS FOR
FURTHER READING

ANSON, P. R. *The Call of the Desert: The Solitary Life in the Christian Church*. London: SPCK, 1973.

BONDI, ROBERTA. *To Love as God Loves: Conversations with the Early Church*. Philadelphia: Fortress Press, 1987.

BOUYER, LOUIS. *The Spirituality of the New Testament and the Fathers*. New York: Seabury Press, 1982.

BURTON-CHRISTIE, DOUGLAS. *The Word in the Desert*. New York: Oxford University Press, 1993.

CASSIAN, JOHN. *Conferences*. Translated by Colm Liubheid. Classics of Western Spirituality. New York: Paulist Press, 1985. This volume contains a wider selection of the Conferences translated in full, with an excellent introduction by Owen Chadwick.

COX, PATRICIA. *Biography in Late Antiquity: A Quest for the Holy Man*. Berkeley: University of California Press, 1983.

DANIELOU, J., and H. MARROU. *The Christian Centuries. Vol. 1: The First Six Hundred Years*. Translated by V. Cronin. New York: McGraw-Hill, 1964.

DOROTHEOS OF GAZA. *Discourses and Sayings*. Translated by Eric Wheeler. Cistercian Studies Series 33. Kalamazoo, Mich.: Cistercian Publications, 1977. As Chrysogonus Waddell said of Dorotheos: "The ideal spiritual master to introduce us into the rich spiritual universe peopled by the denizens of the deserts of Egypt, Palestine and Syria."

EVAGRIUS PONTICUS. *Practikos. Chapters on Prayer*. Translated by John Eudes Bamberger. Cistercian Studies Series 4. Spencer, Mass.: Cistercian Publications, 1970. One of the rare fathers of the desert who was a trained theologian and writer, Evagrius and the whole tradition he represents are ably introduced in this volume by the abbot-psychologist who translated the texts.

EVDOKIMOV, PAUL. *The Struggle with God*. Glenn Rock, N.J.: Paulist Press, 1966.

GRIGGS, C. WILFRED. *Early Egyptian Christianity: From Its Origins to 451 C.E.* Leiden, The Netherlands: E. J. Brill, 1990.

JONES, ALAN. *Soul Making: The Desert Way of Spirituality*. San Francisco: Harper and Row, 1985.

KANNENGIESSER, CHARLES. *Early Christian Spirituality*. Philadelphia: Fortress Press, 1986.

MARKUS, R. A. *The End of Ancient Christianity*. Cambridge, England: Cambridge University Press, 1991.

MERTON, THOMAS. *The Wisdom of the Desert*. New York: New Directions, 1960. A selection of "sayings" introduced and translated in a provocative way by a "father of the desert" of this century.

ROUSSEAU, PHILIP. *Ascetics, Authority, and the Church in the Age of Jerome and Cassian*. Oxford Historical Monographs. Oxford: Oxford University Press, 1978.

————. *Pachomius: The Making of a Community in Fourth-Century Egypt*. Berkeley: University of California Press, 1985.

SPIDLIK, THOMAS. *The Spirituality of the Christian East: A Systematic Handbook*. Translated by A. P. Gythiel. Kalamazoo, Mich.: Cistercian Publications, 1986.

WARD, BENEDICTA. *Harlots of the Desert*. Cistercian Studies Series 106. Kalamazoo, Mich.: Cistercian Publications, 1989. An Oxford scholar and contemplative nun adds to the harlot stories found in this volume and brings an insightful introduction to them.

HELEN WADDELL (1889–1965), author and translator, was born in Tokyo and educated at Victoria College and Queen's University, Belfast, and at Somerville College, Oxford. She was once described as "the Middle Ages' most persuasive interpreter" by the president of Columbia University, where she was a Fellow. She wrote, among others, the books *The Wandering Scholars* (1927), *Medieval Latin Lyrics* (1929), the novel *Peter Abelard* (1933), *Beasts and Saints* (1934), and, in 1936, *The Desert Fathers,* a translation of her own selections from a seventeenth-century Latin collection by Heribert Rosweyde, *Vitae Patrum* ("Lives of the Fathers," 2nd edition, 1628).

M. BASIL PENNINGTON, O.C.S.O., is a Cistercian (Trappist) monk of the Abbey of Our Lady of St. Joseph in Spencer, Massachusetts, presently residing in Our Lady of Joy Monastery, Hong Kong. Born in Brooklyn, he became a monk in 1951 and was one of the *periti* (experts) at the Second Vatican Council. With Thomas Merton he founded Cistercian Publications and pioneered in translating the Cistercian Fathers into English. He is a leading teacher of and writer on a form of contemplative prayer, popularly known as Centering Prayer. Among his numerous articles and 45 books are such classics as *Call to the Center, Thomas Merton—My Brother, A Place Apart,* and *Bernard of Clairvaux.*

JOHN F. THORNTON is a literary agent, former book editor, and the coeditor, with Katharine Washburn, of *Dumbing Down* (1996) and *Tongues of Angels, Tongues of Men: A Book of Sermons* (forthcoming, 1998). He lives in New York City.

SUSAN B. VARENNE is a New York City high-school teacher with a strong avocational interest in and wide experience of spiritual literature (MA, The University of Chicago Divinity School; Ph.D., Columbia University).